SOCIO-ECONOMIC PROFILE OF RURAL INDIA

Volume Four

EASTERN INDIA

Socio-Economic Profile of Rural Inida

Vol. I : SOUTH INDIA
Andhra Pradesh, Karnataka, Kerala, Tamil Nadu

Vol. II : NORTH-EAST INDIA
Assam, Manipur, Tripura, Nagaland

Vol. III: NORTH-CENTRAL & WESTERN INDIA
Punjab, Haryana, Himachal Pradesh, Gujarat, Maharashtra

Vol. IV : EASTERN INDIA
Bihar, West Bengal, Orissa, Uttar Pradesh

About the Editor

Dr. C. Ashokvardhan is an IAS Officer of 1980 Batch and belongs to Bihar cadre. During his career as Indian Administrative Officer, he has been posted in several important Government Departments. Prior to joining Indian Administrative Service, he was teaching in Colleges as a Lecturer in Political Science. He is the author of many books and articles pertaining to issues on Land Reforms, Police Reforms, Agriculture, Rural Development etc. At present he is the Director, Consolidation (Bihar), Government of Bihar.

SOCIO-ECONOMIC PROFILE OF RURAL INDIA

VOLUME FOUR

EASTERN INDIA

(Bihar, West Bengal, Orissa and Uttar Pradesh)

Edited by

C. ASHOKVARDHAN, *I.A.S*

Published for

Centre for Rural Studies

L.B.S. National Academy of Administration, Mussoorie

By

CONCEPT PUBLISHING COMPANY, NEW DELHI-110059

ISBN-13: 978-81-7022-742-7 (Series) **ISBN-10: 81-7022-742-9 (Series)**
ISBN-13: 978-81-8069-605-3 (Vol. 4) **ISBN-10: 81-8069-605-7 (Vol. 4)**

First Edition 2009

Published and Printed by

Concept
Since 1974

Concept Publishing Company

Regd. Office:

A/15-16, Commercial Block, Mohan Garden

New Delhi-110059 (India)

Phones : 25351460, 25351794, *Fax* : 091-11-25357109

Email : publishing@conceptpub.com,
website: www.conceptpub.com

Editorial Office:

H-13, Bali Nagar, New Delhi-110 015, India.

Cataloging in Publication Data--*Courtesy:* D.K. Agencies (P) Ltd. <docinfo@dkagencies.com>

Socio-economic profile of rural India.
v. 4 cm.
Contributed articles. Includes bibliographical references and index.
Contents: v. 4. Eastern India : Bihar, West Bengal, Orissa and Uttar Pradesh /edited by C. Ashokvardhan.
ISBN 13: 9788170227427 (set) ISBN 10: 8170227429 (set)
ISBN 13: 9788180696053 (v. 4) ISBN 10: 8180696057 (v. 4)

1. India--Social conditions. 2. India--Economic conditions. 3. India--Rural conditions. 4. Rural development projects--India. I. Lal Bahadur Shastri National Academy of Administration. Centre for Rural Studies.

DDC 330.954 21

Foreword

India embarked on the process of plan development after its independence. Based on the experience of the last six decades of plan development, there has been paradigm-shift aimed towards achieving inclusive and equitable growth across geographical regions and amongst communities and people. The top-down approach to planning has made way for the concept of democratic decentralization which seeks to tap local needs and resources for planning and execution of development schemes.

Socio economic profile of rural India is regularly published by the Centre for Rural Studies, LBS National Academy of Administration, Mussoorie. These are bâsed on the assignments given to the Officer Trainees. This volume is based on the data collected by them during their training in the district in States of Bihar, West Bengal, Orissa and Uttar Pradesh. These studies cover the entire gamut of rural life in the states and provide valuable insights on the impact of development planning and execution. I hope this volume will prove to be of immense use for Administrators, Academicians and Planners alike.

Rudhra Gangadharan
Director
LBS National Academy of Administration
Mussoorie-248179 (INDIA)

Preface

Development has always had a rather complex matrix. This is more so in the context of Bihar, U.P., West Bengal and Orissa. Simultaneous action is required on multiple fronts to pull the States concerned from the morass of poverty and give to the people a quality of life consistent with human dignity. This requires accelerated growth, creation of gainful employment opportunities, strengthening infrastructure and enhancing human resource development. The relative factor advantages of the eastern region lie in the young demographic profile, fertile soil conditions, abundant water resources and a growing market which can enable value added harnessing of the rich agro-processing potential. The eastern part of the country requires an innovative approach to rejuvenate its water systems and embark on new technologies for an optimum water utilization and conservation.

Improving governance is inextricably linked with enhancing the reach and efficacy of the public delivery system. Besides, accelerated growth must be inclusive for enabling the benefits of development to be shared equitably by all segments of society. This would not be possible without qualitative improvement in human resource development by way of ensuring hundred per cent enrolment for primary education, a sharp decline in dropout ratio, investing in teachers' training and creating additional and more diversified Secondary Vocational Education. Inculcation of skills based on emerging demands is necessary to make the educated employable. Similarly, improvement in the health of the population, apart from welfare gains, has many virtuous circles and enhances productivity. Strengthening infrastructure and making its cost more affordable and more reliable, particularly in roads and power, is central to any growth strategy. This is also critical in shaping perceptions and creating an attractive overall environment for investment as well as harnessing the scope for public-private partnership.

There is large scale disparity of income in the eastern region. The main objective of development is to reduce the disparity in earning among the various sections of the society. It is also imperative to bring into the mainstream those people who belong to the backward communities and classes. Females are lagging behind the men-folk in the fields of education, health and earning. Real development will take place as and when the disparity between men and women, in this regard is reduced/eliminated. Development would also make those people self-dependent for whom this process is unleashed. Also, the people should be empowered enough to choose their own life style.

There are certain limitations of the concept of traditional development and planning:

(a) People who are mostly backward (women, SCs, STs, OBCs and minorities) do not have sufficient awareness about the development and opportunities, since most of them are illiterate. A number of them do not have physical ability to earn their livelihood by dint of hard labour. They are not aware of certain opportunities and services. They are not organized to fight for their rights and benefits. Some of them do not have the interest to change their life style. On the other hand, educated and resourceful people are organized to get most of the benefits of all development and keep on exploiting the most backward people for years together. Their access to social capital is phenomenal.

(b) There is a tendency in our country's development process to make common people more dependent on others instead of giving them the right to lead the development activities on the front. The relations between the coordinators of development and the common people is still a relation between giver and taker. We have failed to inculcate the sense of self-dependence among the large sections of the population.

(c) The villagers themselves are not aware of their vast natural resources and huge labour force. There is also a dearth of joint efforts. Even a few decades ago, the villagers used to take initiative and use their own resources to undertake certain development work. Enough of financial assistance from the government was not available. The villagers themselves used to take initiatives to hold meetings and take decisions to build roads, concretize the embankments of ponds, clean the ponds, raise donations to build schools and repair the existing ones, clean the sewerage canals. But gradually they have started depending on the government and panchayats. The villagers do not realize that most of the money required for the implementation of plans will not come from the government, panchayats and financial institutions. They would have to depend on their own resources. It is still difficult to inculcate the idea that huge amount of unutilized natural resources and labour force could be used to bring change.

(d) Still the people believe that development means building of infrastructure. People are satisfied with the construction of roads and bridges, availability of drinking water, construction of markets and houses. The people associated with planning and the commoners are yet to consider the importance of social developments, like literacy and education, health and hygiene, social security and removal of gender bias.

Needless to say that Bihar, U.P., West Bengal and Orissa have to approach the Eleventh Plan with optimism. It is heartening to note that a process of gradual growth based on state-specific potential has already been set in motion towards the finale of the Tenth Plan. Thus the Eleventh Plan provides the states concerned with a unique opportunity to re-structure policies to achieve a new vision of growth that will be much more broad-based and inclusive.

C. Ashokvardhan

IAS

Contents

List of Tables

Profile of the Contributors

Shri Amarjeet Sinha

Amarjeet Sinha, an IAS officer of 1983 batch, belongs to the Bihar Cadre of Service. Among several responsible positions Shri Amarjeet Sinha has held post of Deputy Director (Senior), Lal Bahadur Shastri National Academy of Administration, Mussoorie. Currently Shri Amarjeet Sinha is the Joint Secretary, Ministry of Health & Family Welfare, Government of India, New Delhi.

Dr. Manabendra Nath Roy

Dr Roy joined the Indian Administrative Service in the year 1980. He served as the District Magistrates in the districts of Jalpaiguri and Midnapore in West Bengal during the period 1988-1993 and also functioned as Ex-Officio Executive Officers of the respective Zilla Parishads. He was Joint Secretary in the Panchayat and Rural Development Department of the Government of West Bengal during the years 1993-1996 and the Commissioner of Commercial Taxes of the State during the period 1997-2002. He is at present the Principal Secretary of the Panchayat and Rural Development Department of the Government of West Bengal and is heading that department since the year 2002. He did his PhD from the Tata Institute of Social Sciences, Mumbai on issues related to Women's Empowerment. His special area of interest is functioning and strengthening of rural local governments, participatory planning at the grassroots level for alleviation of rural poverty and improving delivery of services to the citizen. He has also pioneered the movement for Total Literacy in the district of Midnapore, which was the largest literacy campaign in the country; movement for Total Sanitation and that for organizing the rural women in Self Help Groups for their overall socio-economic development in the state of West Bengal.

Dr. S. Tripathy

Presently he is associated with Entrepreneurship Development Institute of India, Gujarat. He worked as Assistant Professor, Centre for Rural Studies at the LBS National Academy of Administration, Mussoorie for seven years and worked as Researcher in reputed Economic Research Organization for one year. Completed research on rural development, participatory approaches, micro finance, land reforms and the NPO sector. Areas of interest are Econometrics, Micro & Macro Economics and Development Economics.

Shri Jai Singh Shekhawat

Jai Singh Shekhawat is working as a State Programme Manager with National Rural Health Mission in Department of Medical, Health and Family Welfare, Government of Rajasthan. He had completed his Masters in Social Work from Bhopal School of Social Sciences, Bhopal. He was associated with Centre for Rural Studies, Lal Bahadur Shastri National Academy of Administration, Mussoorie as a Research Associate. In CRS-LBSNAA, he prepared several socio-economic State papers based on the village study reports of IAS probationers. He also worked with Indian Institute of Health Management Research, Jaipur as a Research Officer. Mr. Shekhawat has around 3-4 years of research experience in various social and health research projects. His interest areas are Health Management, Rural Development, Data Analysis, Poverty alleviation Programmes and Management Information System (MIS).

Dr. H. C. Pokhriyal

Dr. H.C. Pokhriyal is presently an Executive Director, School of Open Learning, Delhi University. Interests are Decentralized Planning, Special Area Development, Social Sector Programme, Primary

Education and Participatory Rural Appraisal (PRA). He has been associated with International Centre for Mountain Development for conducting collaborative studies. At present he is also a Member of the Working Group on Hill Area Development Programme and Western Ghat Development Programme, constituted by the Planning Commission, Government of India for the Tenth Five Year Plan (2002-2007) period. He was also a member in various appraisal missions in Bihar, Uttaranchal and Tamil Nadu under DPEP. He is a member of the monitoring team for SSA in Uttaranchal.

Dr. C. Ashokvardhan

Dr. C. Ashokvardhan is an IAS Officer of 1980 Batch and belongs to Bihar cadre. During his career as Indian Administrative Officer, he has been posted in several important Government Departments. Prior to joining Indian Administrative Services, he was teaching in Colleges as a Lecturer in Political Science. He is the author of many books and articles pertaining to issues on Land Reforms, Police Reforms, Agriculture, Rural Development etc. At present he is the Principal Secretary, Department of Revenue and Land Reforms, Government of Bihar.

Introduction

C. ASHOKVARDHAN

This volume is the quintessence of the combined efforts of scores of IAS Officer Trainees learning the nuances of rural development, on the spot, in course of their village visits in Bihar, UP, West Bengal and Orissa. This has been the ritual and the rigmarole over the last several years in the LBS National Academy of Administration (LBSNAA), Mussoorie. It later dawned upon the Land Reforms Unit and (now) the Centre for Rural Studies, LBSNAA to glean facts, figures and impressions and the running sinew, region-wise and come out with volumes like this for the benefit of all concerned, instead of pushing the family schedules and alignment reports somewhere in the nook of dark, unvisited cupboards. True, much water has shed since the surveys were carried out. True, the efforts reflect surface realities and hidden truisms stretched over a span of about a decade or so, nevertheless, somewhere a beginning had to be made. Somewhere the perspective had to be captured and trends deciphered. Somewhere suggestions had to come and the vision for tomorrow had to be painted in green in the hue of a newly born sprout, epitomizing hope and a silver lining in a dark cumulonimbus.

Hence, admittedly, this is a rather old, out of tune profile and yet, silhouetted as it is on a note of planning for the future, it is destined to represent a milestone in the march of the states concerned towards the cherished goal of rural uplift and development through well-designed strategies. There one may come across asymmetries, ill planned moves and lopsided outcomes. There might be pointers to regional imbalances. But there is no denying the fact of learning from the past. Judged in this context, a given time frame is outweighed by selecting between a right and a wrong choice, identifying road-blocks, and steer clear through dilemmas and dichotomies inherent in any given approach, whatsoever. There we may discern the funds crunch that is all set to throw the best conceived plans in a disarray.

Nonetheless, more than the money it is the processes that matter eventually. Whether there is a connectivity with the people and (not only a semblance of) participation. Whether those manning the seats of power allow the monolith getting melted and allow devolution. Whether there is a sincere move to empower the unempowered, voiceless and the wronged: questions like these remain the crux. I have every reason to believe that the state papers included in this volume, are not merely a summary of the policies and programmes coming down from the top. The study travels beyond a routine bureaucracy and a routine mindset.

While discussing the rather complex matrix of rural development, the social sector is often lost sight of while social iniquities flourish in the lap of poverty. Bringing families above the poverty line, does not by itself, wave some magic wand, which will remove iniquities. Ages of debris may not be cleared by a stroke of pen. Nevertheless, one could have a structured focus on pockets and hamlets of deprivation, social ostracisation and (criminal) neglect of all concerned. This also has to be ensured that their habitats are clean, diseases are prevented and fought, and the light of education permeates all through unhindered and more than anything else, the gender virus common to both the haves and the have-nots, within the family four walls, is contained and the female segment wins self-respect and self-esteem at a par with the males.

Against the above backdrop, I wish to ponder over certain key issues of the socio-economic profile of Eastern India as reflected in the state papers included in this volume.

HEALTH ISSUES AND POPULATION TRENDS

Bihar

It comes from the Bihar study that there are socio-economic factors among the dalit sections inhibiting a small family. More children mean more hands. Unless the medical and para-medical staff along with other educated people of the villages and through the involvement of panchayats create awareness regarding the family welfare programmes and also provide proper facilities during and after the operations, the small family goals cannot be attained. Further, there is a lack of awareness regarding immunization. It is only once in a while that camps are organized and Sub-Centres are not within reach and there is chronic absence of the full team. On an average, the number of dalits between 50 to 60 years of age and above 60 years is very small indicating thereby that the life expectancy amongst them beyond the age of 50, is quite low. This is because of the kind of strenuous manual labour they undertake, unsupplemented by adequate and healthy diet.

West Bengal

In West Bengal, as far as the growth rate of the population is concerned, only those reports for which survey was conducted after 1991 census had population figures of the villages for both 1981 and 1991 census. The growth rate of population calculated from those reports varied from 12.8 to 48.3 per cent. In one village the population even declined by 9.0 per cent. On an average, the growth rate of population between 1981 and 1991 comes out to be 23.9 per cent. However, as per census report 1991, total population of the State grew at the rate of 24.73 per cent and 23.17 per cent from 1981-91 and 1971-81 respectively. For rural areas alone, the corresponding rates were 23.01 per cent and 20.36 per cent respectively. Growth rate of population in the rural areas of West Bengal had been always higher than the corresponding rate for the entire country right from the decade 1951-61. The total population of the State followed the same trend excepting during the decade 1971-1981 when the population of the State grew at a lower rate than that of the country. The population density of the surveyed villages varied from 232.3 persons per sq. km. to as high as 2628.0 persons per sq. km. in 1981. For villages, for which the 1991 census data was available, such figures varied from 289.1 to 1414.9. The average population density as in 1981 and 1991 was found to be 631.8 persons per sq. km. and 652.8 persons per sq. km. respectively. For the State as a whole the population density as per 1991 census was 767 compared to the national average of 273. Also, West Bengal was the most densely populated State after Kerala till the 1981 census. Due to the higher growth rate of population in West Bengal during 1981-1991 its population density exceeded that of Kerala in 1991.

Common diseases in the villages were those (i) which spread due to insanitary practices and not using safe water; (ii) which occur due to malnutrition; and (iii) vector transmitted diseases like malaria, encephalitis etc. Diseases of the first category like diarrhoea, dysentery, gastro-enteritis were the major causes of illness. Various skin diseases were also common. The six diseases, namely, diphtheria, tetanus, whooping cough, measles, tuberculosis and poliomyelitis were on the decline due to the spread of immunization coverage. However, measles among children and tuberculosis were more common among those six diseases. Incidence of malaria was on the rise. Incidence of snake-bite, road accident, drowning, electrocution and taking poison were the usual causes for un-natural deaths. Maternal mortality rate in those villages was also quite high. Most of the deliveries, particularly in the villages far away from the health centres, occurred under the supervision of the traditional birth attendants (*Dai*). Pre and post-natal care had improved after the opening of health sub-centres under the multipurpose health scheme due to regular supervision of the Health Assistants (Female) who were trained nurses. However, the extent of such supervision varied widely and ante-natal registration was still around 62 per cent. Training of "*Dais*" and higher coverage of pregnant women by tetanus toxoid had also led to some improvement. Maternal mortality rate for the state at present has been estimated to be around 250 to 300 per one lakh live birth.

The Government health infrastructure in the villages centred around the Primary Health Centres (PHCs). However, the distance of the nearest PHC was 5.1 km, on an average, from the surveyed villages. In the worst case the PHC was located at 11 km away. The health sub-centre was normally located nearby and the health workers occasionally visited the villages. Such workers were more useful for mother and child health care programmes and during the spread of epidemics etc. For common ailments people depended more on the village quacks. In cases of major illness ordinary people were not inclined to visit the PHCs. Because of poor communication facilities it was also difficult to take the patients, who were critically ill, to the PHCs. Complicated cases were referred to the Block Primary Health Centres which were normally overcrowded. Few qualified doctors were practicing in the villages or in the nearby towns/growth centres. Fees for consulting such doctors at their chambers was around Rs. 5 while charges for consulting at the patient's residence on call was around Rs. 20. Only two out of all the villages surveyed, one in Darjeeling and the other in the Western region of Midnapore (Binpur-II) had problems of drinking water. The main source of drinking water was tubewell or dugwell. On an average, there was one such spot source for every 23 families. In the worst case 61 families had to depend on only one spot source while in the best case, there was one spot source for every eight families on an average in one village. Only in two villages there was piped water supply and out of those two, one village had only partial coverage. Compared to the above picture in the surveyed villages the position of rural water supply for the State as a whole had only 62 per cent coverage as per the accepted norm (one source per 250 persons). At the beginning of the Eighth Plan (out of the rural population of 493.7 lakh, 308.14 lakh population was fully covered. The source of such coverage was 55.04 lakh by piped water, 211.45 lakh by ordinary spot sources, 41.65 lakh by rig-bored tubewells). Others had only partial coverage. Target coverage for the 8th Plan (1992-97) was 86 per cent of the population and achievement till the end of 1993-94 was nearly 68 per cent. In some of the areas of the State there is serious problem of arsenic contamination. Also there is the problem of salinity in some of the coastal villages. Only a few families in the surveyed villages had toilets and bathrooms. Normally less than 10 per cent of the houses had toilet facilities except in three cases where 32 per cent families had toilets.

Uttar Pradesh and Uttarakhand

In the Bhabar region, the availability of safe drinking water and sanitation is lacking. The major diseases as observed in the study included malaria and typhoid, which occur regularly. The eye disease and jaundice are also found commonly in the region. Moreover the deficiency of iodine has also been observed. It is evident that these diseases are either water-borne or due to the climatic situation in the region. More importantly, these problems can be effectively prevented by improving the existing health services. The medical services were either provided by the auxiliary nurse and midwife (ANM) or the patients have to travel to the nearest town for private medical support. However, vaccination has been administered on regular intervals to the children. The people's perception about the ANM is also not found very satisfactory. Especially, the Scheduled Caste people perceive that the ANM visit is largely confined to the houses of the other (upper) caste people neglecting the SC communities.

In the context of mountain region, the common disease pattern is concerned with typhoid and diarrhoea, which are largely water borne. Interestingly, it has been found that immunization has not been conducted on a regular basis.

A small Ayurvedic dispensary has been located in Raithal village. Although the PHC is established, the quality of health services was found very poor and as reported in the study the doctors do not go to the villages.

The case studies pertaining to Uttar Pradesh and Uttarakhand indicate the need for improving the existing government entitlements concerned with the health services. The regularity in immunizing the target children and conscious efforts on the part of the health staff members (like the ANM) to support the marginal communities in the health entitlements have been realized well. It has also been found that if the potable drinking water and basic sanitation is provided to the people living in the marginal areas, many of the communicable diseases could have been effectively controlled. The essential requirement is to improve the existing health services by efficient management and planning without even a comprehensive understanding about the technical details on medical related aspects. In the context of the preventive side of disease, the role of the development administrator can be visualized in an effective manner.

Orissa

It is unfortunate that many of the health centres in the remote areas exist without any doctor and other supporting staff. People in the tribal villages mostly depend upon their traditional medicine and a quack as consulting a doctor at the time of need is a luxury, which they cannot afford. Non-availability of safe drinking water is mainly responsible for many water borne and other types of diseases. As mentioned in one of the assignments in village Dongasil of Nowrangpur district the availability of safe drinking water despite the inaccessible terrain, has been increasing at a rapid rate in the area, which will certainly reflect in the improved health of the people. The tribals have their own primitive medicinal system in which Jani (Priest) and Desari (soothsayer or astrologer) play an important part.

In fact, at PHC Kashipur, (which provides health services to village Dongasil and other nearby villages), none of the hundred plus patients brought had died. This has quickly spread the message. Now the people have developed good faith in the government hospitals and are bringing the patients wherever the initial symptoms start appearing. As reported in the assignment, village Padwa is not at all planned, the houses are scattered with narrow laces connecting them. Every family drains its garbage and sewage to the street. Hence improvement in the above areas could significantly improve the health conditions of the people. Illicit distillation is done in every house. There are two local varieties of country liquor one made from Ragi and the other from rice, which every family makes in his own house. Many people distill the country liquor hidden in the hills. Previously they used to make it from *Mahua* (a flower), which has been banned. So to de-addict the people, it requires a great effort. In the village study report of the village Rasingtal of Koraput district it is mentioned that there is always an acute shortage of medicines. There are ANM workers and MPHW workers in each village who provide the necessary health services in the village. In the village study report of Betna, it is reported that the Anganwadi centre of the village looks into:

1. Supplementary Nutrition Programme,
2. Immunization,
3. Health Check Up,
4. Referral Services,
5. Health and Nutrition Education, and
6. Non-formal Pre-school Education.

The attendance at the centre is fairly good, and the workers are taking ample interest in their work. Most of the children suffer from malnutrition. From the study report of the Panchayat Karlaguda (Kalahandi) it can be inferred that non-availability of safe drinking water forces villagers to depend upon the same source of water for multiple uses. The villagers bathe, wash and drink in the same stream or tank. The animals also consume water and are washed in the same stream or tank. The people have unhygienic sanitary habits. So many villagers are suffering from water borne diseases.

EDUCATION AND LITERACY

Orissa

Education is an indispensable input for the development of human resources. While the overall literacy rate in 1951 was 15.8 per cent, it was only 4.5 per cent among females. The overall literacy rate in Orissa has increased to 49.1 per cent and that for males to 63.1 per cent and for females to 34.7 per cent as per the 1991 census. Literacy rate among the age group 10-14 is 66.2 per cent and the same in the age group 15-19 is 61.0 per cent, which implies there are drop-outs at the higher level of education. A major factor responsible for the low educational level among females and persons belonging to the Scheduled Castes and Scheduled Tribes is the high drop-out rate at the primary level especially in the tribal and inaccessible areas. The literacy rate of the Scheduled Caste and Scheduled Tribe population was 36.78 per cent and 22.31 per cent respectively according to the 1991 census. Over two decades, i.e. from 1971 to 1991, the literacy rate of females in Orissa has increased tremendously, whereas the literacy rate among the males during the same period has increased at a slightly low pace. This is due to the fact that literacy rate among the females was quite low by the census year 1971. Despite such large increase in the female literacy rate, the gender gap in terms of literacy rate is very high. As mentioned in the assignments though the village Athagadapatna (Ganjam) was declared a totally literate village on 25th October, 1992, there are quite a few gaps between the claims and reality. The literacy rate in the tribal dominated villages is lower as compared to the non-tribal villages. In the village Rasingtal of Koraput the literacy percentage would be around 20 per cent. The literacy percentage among the women as a category is the lowest, around 4 per cent. Further the same among the tribal women is less than 1 per cent. Similarly, in another assignment of village Betna, it is mentioned that literacy is hardly 10 per cent in all the villages together. Education status of household and family members is extremely low. Hardly any member of the family is educated. Only a few children have started going to the school recently. In another report of village Padwa, it is mentioned that the dropout rate is maximum at the primary school level but reduced at high school level. Telugu population do not send their children to school even though they are staying there for quite a long time. Children of the school-going age, who do not attend school, spend their time doing cultivation, herding animals, etc. According to a survey report in Panchayat Karlaguda, Kalahandi there are many lacunae in the education system. The absenteeism of teachers is rampant. In Pastipada village, the school is closed for one month and the teacher comes only to collect his salary. The mid-day meals are not being given regularly. It is in this respect that the role of night schools run by Agragamee, a voluntary agency working in the area, is to be evaluated. The night schools are run by an animator, who is a literate youth from the village teaching in a thatched house constructed by the villagers in the village itself. Solar lights have been provided by the Orissa Renewable Energy Development Agency with the help of Agragamee. The animator gets Rs. 105 per month as remuneration besides study material. The school runs for 2 hours in the evening and students from all age groups are allowed to attend. The adult literacy programme has also very limited impact on the literacy status of the village. It is documented in the village study assignment of village Teleimalti that previously, there were adult literacy centres but with the onset of the total literacy programme they are now non functional.

West Bengal

Coming to West Bengal, the literacy level of the villagers, who were surveyed, varied from 25 to 80 per cent for males and from 3 to 40 per cent for females. Difference of male and female literacy rates varied from around 9 to 25 per cent in different villages. Growth in both male and female literacy rates varied between 9 to 18 per cent from 1981 to 1991.

All the villages studied in West Bengal had primary schools within the village. In those primary schools the number of teachers varied from 2 to 5 and their average number worked out to be 3.5. The teacher target ratio varied from 1:23 to 1:62 and the ratio of male to female students varied from 70:30 to 40:60. However, in most of the classes in different schools the percentage of male students exceeded 50 per cent of the total student strength and enrolment of girls was still lagging behind that for the boys. Overall enrolment of children of the school going age varied from as low as 38 per cent to more than 80 per cent. Attendance of students varied widely from village to village and also over the season in the same village. Such variation was also different for different socio-economic groups. Poverty was one of the main reasons for not sending the children to school. Some of the boys of the school-going age were even employed in other families. Girls who remained out of school remained engaged in household work including looking after the younger siblings. Attendance of girls was reportedly better and more consistent in some of the villages. During peak agricultural seasons the attendance of teachers also declined along with those of the students. Drop-out of students was a serious problem and was as high as 60 per cent in between entry and passing out in primary school in one village. In some of the villages the drop-out was low. The same was generally high for children belonging to the SC & ST communities. The age of the entry of children in schools varied widely and the percentage of over-aged students was high. Annual examination in the primary schools of the State had been abolished and all the children were promoted to higher classes at the end of the academic session. The general impression was that the quality of teaching was not up to the mark and cases had been reported where even a poor family had to engage a tutor for special coaching at home for their children. Physical infrastructure for primary education was not always adequate. Only one primary school had one room and rest of the schools had two to four rooms. Average number of rooms in primary schools in those villages work out to be 2.6. A good number of the schools had *pucca* or semi-*pucca* buildings. Many of those buildings were constructed/improved under various employment generation programmes like NREP, RLEGP or JRY or under the "Operation Black-Board" programme.

Bihar

The study of village Kanwan in the Utlibara Panchayat of Wazirganj Block in Gaya reveals that there is only one primary school located in an old dilapidated building. There are two teachers in the primary school. Fortunately, this was one of the rare schools where the residents did not complain about the absence of teachers from the school. Otherwise this is one of the persistent complaints of the villagers everywhere that the teachers do not attend the school. There is a high school located at a distance of 3 kms., in Rankuppa. The nearest college is at Wazirganj at a distance of 17 kms., 49 per cent of the total school-going eligible children have enrolled in the local primary school. Most of the children who have enrolled in the school are from the upper and backward classes. Amongst the Harijans only

13 per cent of the eligible children have enrolled in the school and even amongst this percentage there is a very high degree of absence from school and a high drop-out rate. On an average 50 per cent of the students were absent doing household job. The drop-out rate after class-5 is very high and out of the 25 students who are in class-5 only 10 had joined the high school. All these 10 students belonged to the upper caste. There is no student attending the college. The literacy rate of the village is 29.8 per cent with the women having a literacy rate of 18.02 per cent. There is no adult education programme running in the village. The village does not boast of any graduate or post-graduate. Dalits are mostly illiterate (1 out of 383 is a matriculate) and their children do not go to the school despite scholarship provided to their parents by the welfare department. One of the main reasons is that the male dalit children have to work along with their parents and children have to look after their younger brothers and sisters. Generation after generation, this trend has been continuing and is one of the main reasons which has kept the dalits in perpetual backwardness. That is why the people from rural areas have not been able to take advantage of the reservation policy. In Kanwan there is not even one dalit family which availed of the facility of reservation in the government jobs.

Uttar Pradesh and Uttarakhand

The Bhabar region case study on the educational entitlements shows that the primary school has been functioning since 1990 and upper primary school was also opened in 1996 in the village. The upper primary school was opened due to the initiatives taken by the local development officer that made the upper primary school accessible in the village to the people. Prior to this the students of the upper primary classes had to travel around 12 km. The school lacks in facilities, like furniture and drinking water. Although the literacy level was found very low in the village and no provision for adult education was available, it is interesting to point out that the children have text books and both the boys and girls including the children from the Scheduled Castes were found equally enrolled in the school. The teacher attendance is an issue and it is observed that out of the two teachers only one is found regular.

The mountain region survey indicates the clustering of the schooling facilities to typically large village. The children from both communities (Scheduled Castes and other castes) were attending the primary school and two teachers teach these children. The upper primary school was also functioning in the village. The higher drop-out of children after completing class-5 is also prominently pointed out in the study. The poor quality of education was reflected at the primary and upper primary schools. The survey points out that the higher drop-out and poor quality of education is mainly due to teachers not taking interest in teaching. The community also is not found aware about the value of education. Very few children were attending the high school.

In Uttarakhand, the efficiency of the schooling system needs considerable improvement. It also highlights the universal enrolment of the children coming from the target child population. However, the drop-out, especially among girls, after the completion of class five has also been observed. The absenteeism of teachers in the primary school is also highlighted in the studies. Low motivation of teachers has also been prominently pointed out in the studies. The people were also found not satisfied with the quality of education imparted in the government schools. Further, the need for addressing the community issues by initiating the proper mobilization and awareness campaign in the marginal areas is well appreciated. More importantly, in the context of improving the quality of education as well enhancing the overall management of schooling system the role of the development administrator is crucial. These issues may be tackled by addressing the motivational issues concerned with the teachers and ensuring the role of the Gram Sabha in micro planning and school management.

The western region case study of the village of Puthi Sarai indicated the positive relationship between the higher level of educational attainment along with the landed assets and income. The education level of the economically poor people and the Scheduled Castes was also found relatively low. It was pointed out that due to low level of education the people were unable to get awareness about various government schemes and development programmes. The study pointed that since the upper caste people have knowledge and economic strength they know the importance of education and send their children to school. The Daulatpur case study shows the regularity in the attendance of teachers in the primary school located in the village. The case study representing the central region covered two primary schools located in two settlements in the Ballopur village. The buildings of the schools also needed repair. The teachers were not found regular in the primary schools resulting into the poor quality of education as the children could not continue the pace of learning. The people were found regular in the primary schools resulting into the poor quality of education as the children should not continue the pace oflearning. The people were found aware about the need of quality education to their children. The study indicated that most of the population is illiterate and therefore, there is an acute need felt by the villagers themselves for non-formal education and adult education. The eastern region is represented by two case studies of village Guwar (Gorakhpur district) and Bar (Sonbhadra district). It is important to mention that both of these villages are dominated by the Scheduled Caste population. However, the Guwar village is mainly representing the feudal agrarian structure. The Bar village is typically showing the peoples' endeavour to improve livelihood in a relatively less fertile land. In the Guwar village, low literacy has been observed. Despite low literacy, people were found more keen in educating their children.

RURAL INFRASTRUCTURE AND BASIC AMENITIES

Orissa

In Orissa, by the end of year 1990-91, only 15 per cent of the total number of villages were connected by all weather approach roads, whereas at the all India level, 41per cent of the six lakh total villages were connected by all weather approach roads. In the developed states like Punjab, Kerala, Haryana, etc. more than 90 per cent of the villages were connected by all weather approach roads by the end of the year 1990-91. Similarly, as evidenced from the census data 1991, 23.5 per cent of people are having electricity connection and 39.1 per cent households are having access to safe drinking water. More than 60 per cent of households in Orissa are not having access to safe drinking water and in rural areas the situation is more serious. Lack of safe drinking water as evidenced by many studies is mainly responsible for several health problems. The socio-institutional factors in combination with the infrastructural problems have produced inadequate fulfilment of the two basic needs of people, among the whole village mass. The widened gap between the villages and towns also arises due to the infrastructural problems found in the villages.

The underdevelopment of non-farm activities in many villages also owes its origin to the underdeveloped infrastructure. The management and maintenance of rural infrastructure created under different employment generation schemes is very poor. Community involvement in the management and maintenance of infrastructure created under different employment generation schemes is very poor. Community involvement in the management and maintenance of infrastructure assets created in the villages must be ensured.

West Bengal

Little more than 40 per cent of the villages surveyed were connected by metalled roads, another 33 per cent of the villages were connected by semi-metalled roads and the remaining villages were connected by *Kuccha* roads. Villages connected with semi-metalled roads were having an average length of around 5 km. of semi-metalled road. Villages connected with *Kuccha* roads were at a distance of around 5.5 km. from metalled/semi-metalled roads. The houses in the villages including those which should be approached by metalled roads were mostly connected by *Kuccha* roads. Hence, during rainy season different houses of the village could be reached only by walking through mud. Buses were plying on most of the metalled roads. Cycles and rickshaws were the common mode of transport and the number of persons using motorcycles was also increasing. The number of bullock carts was decreasing. Railways was also used for travelling longer distances. The distance of nearest railway stations from the surveyed villages varied. Nearly 37 per cent of the villages studied had sub-post offices within the same village. For other villages, the average distance of the post office was around 2.7 km. And the maximum distance was around 6 km. In the State as a whole there were 12 post offices per one lakh population. Average distance of telegraph/telephone facility was around 7 km. and it was as high as 20 km. in one case. Nearly 15 per cent of the villages only had telegraph/telephone facilities within the village. Thus the telecommunication facilities were highly inadequate and the villagers hardly had the scope to use such facilities.

Bihar

A lot has been written about the poor infrastructural facilities in Bihar. The investments that took place in the road construction projects in

North Bihar have been repeatedly washed away by the floods and in other regions, the emergence of a culture of criminal contractors has reduced the efficiency of the works performed. The East-West alignment of the roads was opposite the drainage pattern of North to South. Naturally, a lot of the road infrastructure created under the World Bank assisted Lateral Road Project provided an excellent surface for a few years till they were washed away by the floods. A lot of the expenditure in North Bihar on roads has been washed away on account of the poor planning and coordination with the irrigation engineers in determining the likely alignment of roads. The construction of roads in North Bihar is not the easiest of tasks, given the proneness to floods and therefore, a variant scientific approach was called for, distinct from the road construction norms elsewhere.

There are elements of coercion in the engineering contract systems of Bihar and there are a number of instances where upright engineers have been bumped off for having dared to challenge the supremacy of the contractor. The feudal land armies have now entered the fray of contracts and it is difficult to find a single respectable person going into the work of handling contracts. The heavy public sector investments in the mining areas of Chota Nagpur and the need for transport contracts promoted another form of contracts, symbolized by the legendary racket of sand filling contracts in the coal mining areas. In the power sector, figures reveal that even as late as the early 1970s, Bihar's total installed capacity for power generation compared very well with states like Maharashtra and Andhra Pradesh but the divergence has started since then. By 1991-92, against an installed capacity of 9205 MW in Maharashtra, 4739 MW in Gujarat and 4,223 MW in Andhra Pradesh, Bihar has a mere 1553 MW capacity. A large number of cases like the Kahalgaon NTPC project suffered due to non-acquisition of lands for a long time. The absence of a work culture makes the work of the contractors for these projects very difficult.

FUNCTIONING OF THE PANCHAYATS

West Bengal

The panchayat system was vibrant in all the surveyed villages. The Gram Panchayats were found to be functioning as the first tier of the Government for the village people. All the Gram Panchayats were responsible for the selection of individual beneficiaries, in respective areas, for all individual beneficiary oriented programmes of the government. The Gram Panchayats also collected taxes, although of nominal amount, from the villagers. One Secretary and one job-Assistant apart from a few group "D" employees were serving in the Gram Panchayats. The Panchayats were also responsible for all sorts of emergency relief operations, mobilizing people for participation in various government programmes, organizing literacy movement in respective areas and even sorting out village level problems, quarrels and disputes amongst various groups. Panchayat system was found to have taken deep roots in the village society and was an accepted institution as the local self-government. Most of the Gram Panchayats had their own offices.

Uttar Pradesh and Uttarakhand

The Puthi Sarai case study has been exactly conducted at the time of the beginning of new PRI initiatives. It was found that the villagers took active participation in the election process at the grassroots level.

The Daulatpur case study in the western region (conducted in 1992) also discussed the panchayat related issues and found that the villagers were not conscious about their political right. The study says that the villagers hardly seemed to be conscious of their political rights. There is no participation of the people in the general body meetings of the panchayat. They are not even aware when these meetings take place. The members of gaon panchayat merely sign the resolution prepared by the Pradhan and Village Panchayat Officer. The villagers are very simple and never assert their political rights. They are busy day and night in making their two ends meet. Almost every villager in one voice wanted the separation of village Daulatpur, as a separate gram sabha (GS), from the present GS Akbarpur. The central region case study of a flood prone village already indicated the dichotomy between re-settlers and marginal peasants. In the context of the PRIs, the issue of corruption at the panchayat level was raised. The Kharusa case study in the Bundelkhand region also indicated the slow changes coming in the existing power balances in the village. In the case study the role of gram sabha in identifying the beneficiaries under the rural development programmes has been emphasized. However, on many of the occasions the meetings could not be arranged and paper formalities were completed. The role of the panchayat was confined to implementing JRY and it did not have its own resources.

AGRICULTURE

Bihar

The studies conducted by officers in different parts of the state have all highlighted the extremely high dependence on agriculture. Whereas the incidence of landlessness among the poorer households has been established in the studies on Central and North Bihar, the studies on Chota Nagpur have referred to the availability of lands even with the poor families and the problems arising out of rain-fed agriculture. Given the productivity figures in these reports, there is a large untapped potential in this sector. The governmental programmes have been trying to do something meaningful about it but there is a lot of room for improvement.

A large number of the landed aristocracy, which earlier depended on the government jobs now finds that there are no government jobs anymore. Over large tracts of Mithila such persons are getting back to their lands. The improvement in the private boring irrigation has also spurred growth and there appears to be a tendency to produce more. The labour intensity of paddy cultivation has, however, not been reduced to any significant level. Similarly, breakthrough in rain-fed agricultural practices has also been minimal. The uplands have not shown major increases in productivity, multi-tier cropping or better watershed management. Sufficient recharge is still the greatest challenge for sustainable agricultural development. We are still not using appropriate agronomical practices to make better use of the available soil moisture. Vegetables like tomato, brinjal, beans etc. can grow well even with limited soil moisture in rain-fed conditions.

The Eastern U.P.-Bihar region is yet to make the great leap forward while agro-climatically it can be the "rice bowl of the nation". The land reforms measures have failed to promote productivity. Tenancies continue to be insecure. Though owner cultivators have applied innovative methods in some districts, the region as a whole is yet to reap the benefits of land reforms and secure tenancies as an incentive to produce more. The rhetoric of land reforms has not been able to project its economic necessity. Absentee landlordism of a fragmented and neglected kind is this area's greatest bane. Fast changing agricultural technologies require meaningful extension work. Training and orientation of field functionaries and improving their motivation, is urgently required.

The reports of the IAS Officer Trainees have clearly established the skewed distribution of lands and how certain caste oligarchies hold sway over the agricultural operations. The fragmentation of lands and absence of consolidation have also been pointed out in some reports. It is important to realize that for any major breakthrough in agriculture, security of tenancies and the "land to the tiller" are essential prerequisites. It is the cultivator who must gain from innovations and production and the systems of crop sharing must be worked out in a non-usurious way. Credit for agriculture also has a class character in Bihar and unless and until we reform the entire cooperative network, it will be difficult to reach out to the most needy farmers. In the Chota Nagpur-Santhal Pargana regions, the poor tribals still own land and it is, therefore, possible to do something in the primary sector of agriculture and aquaculture. The harvesting of rain water is the greatest challenge in these regions.

Reports of all the IAS Probationers have pointed out the very high dependence on agriculture in villages. They have all argued for diversification. The absence of processing units as also the systematic development of secondary and tertiary sectors has been pointed out by the Officer Trainees.

Uttar Pradesh and Uttarakhand

It has been pointed out in the study of Puthi Sarai that the seeds and fertilizers were generally accessible from the cooperative stores and under the present situation the role of money lenders has been drastically reduced. The surplus grain is sold in both the government purchasing centres and in the private market. The case study of Daulatpur village in Etawa district did not calculate the surplus generation, but discussed the availability and use of seeds and fertilizers by the farmers. The case study shows that around sixty per cent of the seeds are grown by the farmers themselves. The farmers use chemical fertilizers. The cooperative societies are found working on the supply side. However, it has been reported that the availability of fertilizers in the right quantity and at the right time is an issue for the poor peasants in the villages. The case study of Ballopur in Barabanki district of central region pointed out the location of the village on the flood plain area of river Ghagra. The study shows that due to flood prone area of the river the farmers largely remained at the subsistence level as usually one crop was lost due to flood. Significantly, due to flood the land gets extra enrichment and becomes very fertile, and in majority of the cases a relatively higher level of production of single crop was observed that makes the farmers stick to the land despite the problem of floods.

Orissa

The base of the village economy in Orissa is agriculture. Agriculture is mainly subsistence oriented and rain fed in a scenario of intensive use of primitive and traditional technology. Around 60 per cent of cultivable land is rain-fed and single crop paddy is grown in the best quality land and pulses and oil seeds like gram, *arhar*, *til*, mustard, groundnut, etc. are grown in the upland. Due to population pressure, it is found that most of the cultivators in Orissa are marginal farmers (around 80%) owning less than 2 acres of land. The yield rate of paddy is invariably low except some developed pockets of irrigated area in Puri, Cuttack, Sambalpur, Bargarh and Sonepur districts.

It has been observed that the share of agriculture in the net state domestic products has been declining in Orissa. However, the pace of fall in the contribution of agriculture during 1983–1993 is slower in the state as compared to the nation as a whole. The most contradictory fact is that in spite of a fall in the share of agriculture in SDP, the percentage of population engaged in agriculture has not gone down and it has remained stagnant with a minor decline since the mid-sixties. The productivity levels of major crops have not seen any change. Rather many double cropping areas have been brought under the single cropping system. Commercialization and mechanization of agriculture have taken place in a very limited manner. All these are mainly responsible for the fall in the share of the agriculture sector. Definitely the rise in service sectors and other sectors' contribution is also a reason for the fall in the share of the agriculture sector. But the growth of other sectors has not resulted in fall in the dependency on agriculture.

West Bengal

Aman paddy, sown in Kharif season, was the most important crop in all the villages surveyed. Other important crops were *aus* paddy, *boro* paddy, *jute*, wheat, potato, other vegetables, mustard, *til*, various pulses etc. Cultivation of sugarcane, maize, groundnut, *arhar* etc. was also reported from some of the villages. Around 80 per cent of the area under cultivation was used for foodgrain production and out of the total area for foodgrain production more than 80 per cent is used for producing rice. Depending on the agro-climatic condition, use of irrigation, improved seeds and application of other inputs, productivity of crops varied widely.

Cropping intensity in the villages studied varied widely from 105.0 to 250.0. Average cropping intensity worked out to be 177. However, for the state as a whole the cropping intensity target by the terminal year of the Eighth Five Year Plan (1996-97) is 162 and the same was estimated to be around 150 during 1993-94. Seeds were reported to be procured from the following sources: (a) farmer's own seeds, (b) private dealers, (c) government agencies/farm/mini-kits. Farmers were cautious about the quality of seeds and the use of improved/high-yielding varieties (HYV) seeds were encouraged. *Boro* paddy was cultivated with HYV seeds only while 20-40 per cent of *Aman* paddy was cultivated through HYV seeds. Use of HYV seeds depended on the availability of irrigation facilities and credit required for applying higher dose of fertilizer for those crops. Use of HYV seeds was also very high for potato, wheat and vegetables. Use of chemical fertilizer, particularly in crops like Boro paddy and potato was very common. In fact farmers were aware of the effect of chemical fertilizers particularly for HYV seeds. In many cases arranging money for purchasing fertilizer was a constraint. Testing of soil for the application of balanced dose of fertilizer was also reported from quite a few villages. Cow-dung was normally applied and nearly half of the cow-dung produced in the villages was used as manure while the remaining half was burnt away. The dose of cow-dung applied per acre varied from 10 Q to 30 Q. The use of green-manure was not so common.

Wet and semi-wet methods of cultivation were followed for paddy. While *Aman* and *Boro* paddy were transplanted in lines, the autumn paddy was usually broadcasted. Traditional ploughs were most commonly used for cultivation. It required around 3 ploughs (8 hours a day) for cultivating 1 acre of wet land. The requirement per acre of dry land was 5 ploughs. Use of power tillers was also reported from some of the villages. Threshers, hand operated sprayers and dusters were very common. The pump-sets used for irrigation were mostly diesel operated. Traditional water-lifting devices like *donga/dungi* (a canoe shaped vessel), were used by the poor cultivators. Irrigation was in high demand among the farmers. General prosperity of the villages depended substantially on the spread of irrigation. Farmers were very keen to arrange for minor irrigation sources. The main thrust was on exploiting ground water by sinking shallow tube-wells. Where water was not available easily, the farmers, particularly the richer sections opted for submersible pumps. The demand for getting sufficient water for *Boro*-paddy cultivation was very high. High level of exploitation of ground water occasionally led to drinking water crisis in some areas during the peak summer. There were also quite a few government deep tube-wells in the surveyed villages. Water tax for irrigation from the government sources was very low. The rate of irrigation of one acre of land was Rs. 60 for *Aman* paddy, Rs. 240 for *Boro* paddy, Rs. 60 for Wheat, Rs. 60 for Jute. For irrigation from private sources for *Boro* paddy, the rate worked out to be around Rs. 800 per acre.

RURAL DEVELOPMENT

Orissa

In spite of consistent efforts of the state government during the last four decades the percentage of population below the poverty line of the state has remained higher than the same at the all India level. Orissa is held to be the poorest state in India. Within the state also regional disparity in terms of backwardness is quite acute. Western and southern Orissa has been associated with relatively more backwardness and higher concentration of poverty. In the rural areas of the state, the percentage of population below poverty line increased from 67.28 per cent in the year 1973-74 to 72.32 per cent by the year 1977-78, whereas at the national level poverty has declined during the same period. The peculiar nature of the state is that most of the poor people in the rural areas are not able to manage the minimum food requirement. This is evidenced by the fact that in the southern parts of the state there have been reports of starvation deaths. The poor performance of agriculture along with lack of industrial growth seems to be the most important cause of poverty.

From the regional clustering of districts it seems southern region is quite homogenous in the sense that all the districts of the region are having high poverty incidences. But in the more heterogeneous northern region, Kendujhar and Mayurbhanj are the poorest districts. Another thing is that the fall in the incidences of poverty has taken place in the coastal and northern regions, whereas in the case of the southern region, poverty has increased over the years 1983-84 to 1987-88. The main reason behind such high incidence of poverty in the southern parts of the state is the high concentration of tribal people in this region. Poverty is acute among the tribal people living in the rural areas.

The incidence of poverty is generally very high among the socially and economically backward sections of the society. It is more severe among the Scheduled Tribes and the Scheduled Castes. The percentage of the ST population of the state below poverty line is the highest among all the social groups and it is followed by the SC population.

It has been observed in the village studies that the rural development and poverty alleviation programmes created some employment for the poor and the landless every year. The assistance from the government in the form of subsidies has made the people complacent. They feel that the government must help them out of the trouble they are in.

West Bengal

The important poverty alleviation programmes under implementation in the villages were NREP (National Rural Employment Programme) and RLEGP (Rural Landless Employment Guarantee Programme) etc. NREP and RLEGP were merged into one programme called (Jawahar Rozgar Yojana (JRY) by the Government India with effect from 1989-90. Other important programmes under implementation for the weaker sections were the Special Component Plan for the Scheduled Castes (SCP) and the Tribal Sub-Plan (TSP) for the Scheduled Tribes.

As per reports, employment generation programmes like the National Rural Employment Programme (NREP), the Rural Landless Employment Guarantee Programme (RLEGP), and the Jawahar Rozgar

Yojana (JRY) were implemented in all the villages. Works usually taken up under the programmes were found to be: the construction and maintenance of roads; the construction of school buildings, *anganwadi* centres, excavation of tanks, wells, canals, social forestry, construction of field channels, sinking of tube-wells/drinking water wells, the construction of huts, the construction of rest sheds etc. Huts were also constructed under the Indira Awas Yojana (IAY), a sub-programme of the JRY. Assets found in the villages were, in general, of good quality. In a few cases, the construction of *kuccha* roads was found to be washed away subsequently in the rains. Semi-metalled or *Kuccha* roads and social forestry works were the most common assets created in the villages out of those programmes. Extension of minor irrigation and primary school construction were other areas of success.

Wage-employment received by different families through such programmes, in the surveyed villages, varied from a few days to 45 days in a year. 4.9 per cent of the surveyed SC & ST families had got their houses constructed under IAY. The houses were occupied and were of good quality.

In the State as a whole, 558.81 lakh man-days were generated under the JRY during 1989-90. This was the highest achievement for mandays generation in the State during the period of survey. As in 1991 there were 48.7 lakh agricultural labourers in the State. As per concurrent evaluation conducted by the Government of India in between January and December 1992, 64.1 per cent of the employment generation was done through the landless labourers. Employment generation by the landless labourers during 1989-90 was 358.2 lakh man-days. Employment generation by each landless labourer in that year works out to be 7.4 man-days on an average. A family having two workers got around 15 days of employment on an average. 93,092 houses were constructed under the IAY, programme up to 1992-93. Till then the programme was confined to the SC & ST families only and the coverage of families in the entire State worked out to be around 6.5 per cent compared to 4.9 per cent as found in the villages surveyed.

All the villages had some IRDP beneficiaries. The total number of such beneficiaries, types of schemes implemented, etc. varied from village to village. The beneficiaries were always selected by the Panchayats and only deserving families were extended assistance under the programme. Selection of beneficiaries, who were otherwise ineligible, on political consideration, was reported from a number of villages. Generally traditional schemes were selected and augmentation of income was not always sufficient to raise the families above poverty line. Loss of assets was reported in a few cases. In the remaining cases, the economic conditions of the families improved, though marginally. All villages normally had some enterprises like a tea stall, a grocery shop, a tailoring unit, house dairy, poultry, carpentry etc. established under the IRDP. Sometimes there were a number of similar enterprises leading to competition amongst each other and sharing of business within a limited market. Assistance for minor irrigation activities like providing pump-set, free boring etc. was reported to be very useful. Amongst the service sector, plying of rickshaws, cycle repairing shops etc. were common. Quantum of assistance was not high and was one of the reasons for insufficient income augmentation. There were also cases of under-financing. Few cases were reported where no assets were created. In a few cases money was used for some other purpose or even kept in banks. The beneficiaries were not always having sufficient awareness about IRDP as a business enterprise for augmenting their income. In some cases, poor entrepreneurship was the problem behind the limited success of the programme. Some people even considered the assistance as a grant and repayment of the loan was not considered a duty. The position of recovery was generally not good. Delay in the disbursement of bank loan was another problem resulting in the poor quality of the implementation of the programme.

Bihar

A focus has built on the proper selection of projects keeping in view their viability and feasibility and provision of forward and backward linkages. While not denying their importance, it is desirable to emphasise two areas of concern that are crucial for improving the repayment position of IRDP loans.

(a) The suppliers of IRDP assets usually hand over assets of inferior quality to the beneficiaries, taking advantage of their ignorance, illiteracy and poverty. Such assets have a shorter life and require frequent repairs involving considerable expenditure. Naturally, the repayment is affected. The remedy is to keep constant vigil and maintain pressure for supplying quality goods.

(b) People, in general, have developed an attitude of non-payment of the government and bank dues. They have to be educated that every loan is given for a purpose and that the same money which is repaid has to be recycled. Better follow-up and recovery efforts will also ensure better response in repayment. Sadly, banks seem to loose contact with the beneficiaries once the loan is given. By reverse action, frequent contacts with beneficiaries for ensuring repayment will also motivate them for making better use of their assets and earning more so as to enable them to use a part of the earnings for repayment.

VILLAGE INDUSTRIES AND TRADE

West Bengal

The largest number of rural artisans in the villages were the weavers. According to the National Handloom Census conducted during 1987-88, there were 3,38,499 looms in the State giving full/partial employment to 7,11,563 persons. Other common artisans were the carpenters, blacksmiths, potters, sweat-meat producers, gold and silver smiths, cobblers, bell-metal workers, "dokra workers", stone carving and wood carving workers, conch-shell workers, mat weavers, *bidi*-workers, manufacturers of various horn products etc. Other trades in which more and more people were getting engaged were sericulture, lac manufacturing, tailoring, rope-making, *muri* (puffed rice) making, wheat crushing, de-husking of paddy, mustard oil mill, bakery, boat making, cycle repairing, radio repairing, repairing of agricultural implements etc. All the villages surveyed had the existence of various types of village household industries. Many of the artisans were very poor and were somehow eking out their lives. The younger generation of their families was not always keen to join their family traditions because of the lower economic viabilities of such activities. Those who joined had hardly any other option. In the State as a whole, as per the 1991 census, there were 8.04 lakh household industries out of which 6.38 lakh were in the rural areas. Thus a little more than 4 per cent of the rural households had their main earnings out of household industries. Cottage and small scale industries, which were promoted by the district Industries Centres, also provided large number of employment. As on 31 March, 1993 there were 4.09 lakh registered units in the State and estimated employment was around 27 lakhs.

Apart from the growth of business related to agricultural produce and supply of inputs related to agriculture and allied activities, some business activities like tea-stalls, grocery, stationery shops, ration shops, ready made garment selling, small hotels (on the roadside) etc. were increasing in the rural areas. Some of the petty traders did not have fixed shops but they sold their items in various daily markets or by hawking in villages, at nearby bus stations or even in trains.

The contributors to this volume hold a reputation in their own right as sagacious administrators and research scholars. They have endeavoured to decipher the labyrinth of rural development in the study area within the framework delineated for village surveys and also beyond. They have tried to build state perspectives in the areas concerned and have connected the findings in the sample villages to the broad spectrum of development in the state as whole. While Shri H. C. Pokhriyal, Shri S. Tripathy and Shri Jai Singh Shekhawat are social scientists representing academics, Dr. M. N. Roy, IAS, my batch-mate (West Bengal: 1980) carries a nation-wide reputation in introducing grass-roots level planning in West Bengal, a pioneer move in the country by itself. Shri Amarjeet Sinha, IAS had a stint in the LBSNAA, Mussoorie and is well-known for his fervour for elementary education.

In a nutshell, the rather raw, first-hand experience penned down by the fresh entrants in the superior civil services has been touched up by subject-matter specialists and that makes the portrait of East India's rural scenario complete.

The publication further epitomizes the patronage received from Shri Rudhra Gangadharan IAS, Director and Shri Padamvir Singh, Joint Director, LBSNAA, Mussoorie. It also remains a testimony to the unswerving zeal of Shri Yatendra Kumar IAS, Deputy Director (Sr.) & Co-ordinator, Centre for Rural Studies and Dr. B. Ashok IAS, Deputy Director and Alternate Co-ordinator, Centre for Rural Studies, LBSNAA, Mussoorie and of Dr. Varunendra V. Singh, Research Associate and the whole team in the CRS, by which the painstaking socio-economic survey reports have been encapsulated and presented to the practicing as well as the academic world.

Finally, through the plethora of debates, and discussions, there has been a late convergence of opinion that rural development to come through has got to be a two-way traffic. The tree is not to be missed for the wood. The people have to take up the cudgels in the long run and have to chalk out a destiny and a road-map for themselves.

1

Bihar

AMARJEET SINHA

GROWTH TRENDS

The trend in the growth rate of Bihar's Gross State Domestic Product (GSDP) during the Tenth Plan has been volatile, mainly because of the dominance of the agricultural sector in the state's economy (Table 1.1). During this period, against an average growth rate of 7 per cent for the Indian economy, Bihar's average annual growth rate was 4.01 per cent.

Table 1.1: Trends in Bihar's Gross State Domestic Product (Ninth & Tenth Plans)

Year	*State Domestic Product (lakh Rs.)*	*Change over Previous Year (%)*	*Annual Average Growth Rate (constant 1993-94) Prices (%)*
1997-98	2592076	(-) 3.85	3.25
1998-99	2788792	7.59	4.10
1999-2000	2891397	3.68	4.03
2000-01	3450098	19.32	6.09
2001-02	3125936	(-) 9.40	4.02
2002-03	3615961	15.68	5.25
2003-04 (P)	3290950	(-) 8.98	3.73
2004-05 (Q)	3688196	12.07	4.46
2005-06 (A)	3619819	(-) 1.85	3.92

Note: P: Provisional, Q: Quick Estimate, A: Advanced Estimate

During the Tenth Plan, Bihar's economy grew at a rate that was marginally higher than its growth rate in the Ninth Plan period and even its per capita income just crept up. However, the state's growth rates have been low compared to the national average (Table 1.2).

Table 1.2: Growth in Income and GSDP: Bihar *vs.* India (Ninth & Tenth Plans)

	Ninth Plan		*Tenth Plan*		*(2001-02 to 2004-05)**	
	India	*Bihar*	*India*	*Bihar*	*India*	*Bihar*
Per capita GDP growth rate	4.00	1.00	5.50	2.00	NA	NA
Growth in GDP of which	5.50	2.90	7.00	4.01	6.45	5.67
(a) Agriculture	2.00	(-) 1.14	1.80	0.96	1.03	5.01
(b) Industry	4.60	7.53	8.00	9.80	6.96	10.58
(c) Services	8.10	6.37	8.90	5.08	8.64	5.12

* According to Planning Commission CAGR 3 Years

The bifurcation of the state in 2000 had an impact on the structure of the economy: the state of Jharkhand was created from the industrially advanced and mineral-rich southern-half of the state. While 46 per cent of the land area was transferred to Jharkhand, 75 per cent of the population remained with Bihar, leading to an increase in population density in the latter. The contribution of the secondary sector, which was 15.39 per cent in 1980-81, rose to 20.98 per cent in 1990-91 and fell to 10.55 per cent in 2000-01, less than half the share of the secondary sector nation-wide which is around 25 per cent.

The tertiary sector has grown disproportionately and without concomitant in the secondary sector. Its contribution was 25.84 per cent in 1980-81, but its high growth in the 1990s raised its contribution to 49.77 per cent of SDP in 2000-01, which is at par with the country at large.

In the year 2004-05, the contribution of Agriculture, Industry and Services Sectors in GSDP at 1993-94 prices was 40, 12 and 48 per cent respectively as against 20, 27 and 53 per cent respectively at 1999-2000 prices for the country as a whole.

In spite of the efforts of planned development in the past several decades, the regional disparities have widened and several states like

Bihar are at the lowest rung of the development indicators. Infrastructural developments like roads, power, health and sanitation and other socio-economic indicators are abnormally poor compared to the developed states. The backwardness of Bihar is due to historical reasons—low per capita plan expenditure, inadequate central assistance, recurrence of floods and droughts, low C-D ratio, etc. The bifurcation of the state has added further miseries to it. With 46 per cent of land transferred to Jharkhand, it has to sustain 75 per cent of the population of the undivided state, leading to an extremely high density of population. The land area transferred to Jharkhand was very rich in mineral wealth, power plants, industrial units and human development institutions. The bifurcation of the state has had its impact on income and revenue raising capacity of the state and consequent fall in the State Domestic Product has been of the order of 40 per cent while revenue receipts have fallen by 33 per cent. As a result of bifurcation, the state has become deficient in natural resources and minerals including coal which has impeded its industrial development. For a long term solution of this problem of energy deficiency, the state should be assigned mining blocks and not mere coal linkages. The National Plan should look into this problem in order to bring Bihar on the targeted industrial growth path.

ELEVENTH PLAN OBJECTIVES

Bihar has a lot of catching up to do, and it has to do this rapidly. If the economies of Bihar and the country continue to grow at their respective Tenth Plan rates during the Eleventh Plan period, the per capita income of Bihar in 2013-14 will be Rs. 5589 and India's would be Rs. 23209. In this scenario, at the end of the decade, India's per capita income will be 4.15 times of Bihar's per capita income. Thus the gap has to be bridged by a significant increase in the growth rate and a pattern of growth which can permeate its benefits to all sections of the society. In Bihar's context, the Eleventh Plan mantra is all inclusive growth at an accelerated pace, accompanied by improved delivery of social services.

Inclusive Growth: Reducing the Poverty Headcount

Even after the formation of Jharkhand, Bihar remains the third most populous state in the country with 83 million people. Around 40 per cent of the population is below the poverty line, which is the highest in the country. As per Planning Commission figures of 1999-2000, rural poverty (44.3%) was substantially higher than urban (24.7%), but with 9 out of every 10 persons in Bihar living in villages, poverty in Bihar is significantly a rural phenomenon. The rural poor have limited access to land and livestock, education (80 per cent of the bottom quintile household's heads have no education), health care, and well-paid jobs. Their main source of income is agricultural wages or casual non-farm jobs. A large percentage of them are landless or near-landless, the livestock they own is of poor stock, and they are often denied opportunities for social reasons, such as caste.

The State managed to reduce its poverty levels during the 1990s (1993-94 to 1999-2000) by about 7 percentage points, but this was far below the national average. Bihar's HDI rank among the states has remained unchanged at 15 since 1981, while its score increased marginally from 0.237 in 1981 to 0.308 in 1991 and then fell to 0.267 in 2001.

Rapid growth has to be an essential part of the strategy since it is only in a rapidly growing economy that incomes of the majority of the population will be raised sufficiently to bring about a general improvement in living conditions. Further, the country's own experience with growth throws up some lessons for Bihar. Accelerated GDP growth in India during the 1990s did not ensure a similar growth in employment. According to NSS (large sample) data, the rate of rural unemployment (current daily status) increased from 5.6 per cent in 1993-94 to 7.1 per cent in 1999-2000 and from 7.4 to 7.7 per cent in urban areas. Thus, along with faster and more equitable growth, sustained and gainful employment generation at a faster pace to tackle the unemployment backlog—will be one of Bihar's key goals for the Eleventh Plan. Vigorous efforts will be needed to create an investment-friendly environment in labour-intensive sectors such as agriculture, animal husbandry, MSEs and the services sector.

Social Delivery: Access to Services for All

Education and good health are essential to empower people to be productively employed in their future. The state's poor social indicators underline the importance of improving access to essential public services, especially education and health (Table 1.3). Educational indicators for Bihar are abysmally low compared to the national average, largely because of the lack of educational institutions and staff. Poor delivery of education has resulted in a high degree of migration from the state for education and employment, resulting in a large and continuous loss of human potential. The situation is almost identical in health service delivery, where the shortage in medical personnel and physical infrastructure are far higher than the national norms. The entire social delivery system covering *anganwadis*, ration shops, schools, hospitals and so on, needs substantial inputs and improved efficiency to be rejuvenated and made purposive. A World Bank study indicates that at the present rate of progress, by 2015, Bihar will be able to achieve only two (reduction in child malnutrition and access to safe drinking water) of the eight Millennium Development Goals. These can only be accelerated if the social sectors receive substantial investment during the Eleventh Plan.

At the same time, social services will have to be well targeted and responsive to the community's needs. There is sufficient evidence to show that funds are not the binding constraint to improving the delivery of services; rather it is the implementation capacity of the delivering agencies and appropriate monitoring of outcomes.

Table 1.3: Development and Demographic Indicators

Indicators	*Bihar*	*India*
Total population (million)*	83.0	1028.8
Population (rural) (%)*	89.6	72.2
Birth rate**	30	24
Child population (0-4 years) (million)*	11.0	110.4
Sex ratio (all)*	921	932
Sex ratio (0-6 years)*	942	927
Literacy rate (total) (%)*	46.96	64.59
Literacy rate (females) (%)*	33.12	53.67
Life expectancy at birth: male***	61.4	61.6
Life expectancy at birth: female***	59.5	63.3
Infant mortality rate**	61	58
Underweight children (below 3 years) (%)	54.4	47.0
Gross enrolment ratio (6-14 years) (%)	47	65
Complete immunization (all) (before 24 months) (%)	12.8	56.6
Maternal mortality rate (MMR)	371	301

* Census 2001

** 2003-05, SRS

*** 1998-02 (CSO)

Growth Potential in the Eleventh Plan

The low growth of Bihar's GSDP compared to the national average can be attributed to the low accumulation of physical capital and lack of efficiency in the use of capital. From 1999-2000 to 2003-04, the investment rate has been around 27 per cent for the country, against which Bihar's average rate of investment was abysmally low at 15 per cent of GSDP (see Table 1.4). Of this, private investment as a percentage of total investment for the state was on average 59 per cent.

Table 1.4: Trends in the Rate of Investment (% of GSDP)

Year	*Public*	*Private*	*Total*
1999-2000	6.72	8.97	15.69
2000-2001	5.28	8.79	14.07
2001-2002	5.68	8.58	14.26
2002-2003	4.70	8.94	15.64
2003-2004	8.55	9.86	18.41

The Planning Commission has projected an average growth rate close to 9.0 per cent with acceleration through the plan period to end with a rate of around 10 per cent during the Eleventh Plan. For Bihar, four rates of growth of SDP at 7 per cent, 8.5 per cent, 9 per cent and 10 per cent have been assumed for working out different investment scenarios in the Eleventh Plan. Table 1.5 presents an assessment of investment requirements in Bihar for these target growth rates, which will call for varying average rates of investment, public and private.

Table 1.5: Alternative Investment Scenarios for the Eleventh Plan

(Per cent)

Target rate of growth	7	8.5	9	10
Average investment rate	19.72	23.65	24.95	27.52
Public investment as % of GSDP	6.90	8.28	8.73	9.63
Private investment as % of GSDP	12.82	15.37	16.22	17.89

For Bihar, acceleration from per cent growth to 10 per cent will require an increase in the total investment rate from 19.72 to 27.52 per cent. The scale of the increased investment is substantial and will have to be financed by increased domestic and government saving.

These different growth scenarios give rise to alternative estimates of GSDP for the state economy (Table 1.6).

Table 1.6: Projected Eleventh Plan SDP at Alternative Growth Rates

(Rs. crore at 2006-07 prices)

Year	State Domestic Product			
	7% rate of growth	*8.5% rate of growth*	*9% rate of growth*	*10% rate of growth*
2007-08	70784	71776	72107	72769
2008-09	75739	77877	78597	80046
2009-10	81041	84497	85671	88050
2010-11	86714	91679	93381	96855
2011-12	92784	99472	101785	106541

The Incremental Capital Output Ratio

Based on data on capital formation in the state for the period 1999-2000 to 2003-04 and data on SDP with a lag of two years, the incremental capital-output ratio (ICOR) for major sectors works out to 2.78 (Table 1.7).

Table 1.7: ICOR by Broad Sector (1999-2004)

Sl. No.	*Sector*	*ICOR*
1.	Agriculture and allied activities	3.36
2.	Industry	4.66
	2.1 Mining, manufacturing and construction	4.54
	2.2 Power, water supply and gas	5.04
3.	Services	2.18
	3.1 Transport and communications	5.99
	3.2 Others, including social services	1.02
	All Sectors	2.78

In the Eleventh Plan for Bihar the ICOR can be realistically assumed to be higher than the ICOR for 1999-2004, at 3.0 as the state will be incurring vastly higher capital expenditures on developing infrastructure projects in roads, bridges, power, irrigation and flood control.

Based on this postulated ICOR, proposed outlays for the Eleventh Plan for the alternative rates of growth have been estimated (Table 1.8).

Table 1.8: Projected Eleventh Plan Outlays at Alternative Growth Rates

(Rs. crores)

Rate of Growth (%)	Proposed Outlay		
	Public	Private	Total
7.0	46600	86551	133151
8.5	58310	108282	166593
9.0	62355	115804	178159
10.0	70680	131257	201937

With the recent encouraging spurt in private investment, a moderately higher proportion of 65 per cent has been assumed for the Eleventh Plan. It may be recalled that the Planning Commission has assumed the share of the private sector in the total investment in the country to be 70 per cent. The projected outlay for the Eleventh Plan estimated at Rs. 58310 crore would enable the state to grow at 8.5 per cent. The loan component of this outlay is calculated and pegged in conformity with the physical correction path under the FRBM Act.

Focus on Agriculture and Allied Sectors: Core Competence

Agriculture is the core competence of the state. In the 1980s, Bihar's agricultural growth rate of 4.6 per cent was above the national average, but this plummeted between 1991-92 and 1995-96 to 2 per cent. While growth rates have revived somewhat in recent years, agricultural productivity remains below its potential. Given the high proportion of workforce engaged in agriculture, its large share in the GSDP, and the high incidence of rural poverty, the Eleventh Plan's emphasis will need to be on agriculture and allied services to effectively reduce rural poverty and fuel growth in other sectors.

Bihar has enough potential in agriculture to address the short-term concerns over food security of the country. To realize this potential, the Eleventh Plan will place greater emphasis on agricultural extension, crop diversification, increased yields from rainfed agriculture (which accounts for 62 per cent of cultivable land), and narrowing the demand-supply gap in animal products. Sustained agricultural growth will be based on a rapidly expanding food-processing industry, rejuvenation of irrigation infrastructure, a network of farm roads, better marketing of farm products and flow of agricultural growth like land reforms and tenancy relations need to be addressed. Therefore, the Eleventh Plan will be based on a holistic model for agricultural development, at the end of which the state will transit to a self-sufficient state in food grains.

Bihar: Main Reasons for Low Crop Productivity

Poor Quality Supply of Inputs

- The lack of an assured, timely supply of quality seeds for high yielding varieties, and hybrid varieties. Seeds of high yielding varieties have been critical in increasing crop production. Dwarf gene of rice and wheat did wonders in the 1960s as these varieties were short-statured and could respond well to fertilizers, irrigation and other management practices. The development of hybrid varieties in many crops opened yet another opportunity to further increase crop production and productivity.
- Low and regionally unbalanced fertilizer use: The present level of fertilizer application in the state is 98 kg/ha whereas it is more than 175 kg/ha in Punjab.
- Lack of access to credit (this has hindered, among other things, the adoption of technology, as an example, for 104 lakh farm holdings in the state, there are only 20 lakh Kisan credit cards).

Agricultural Practices

- *Lack of mechanization:* Farm techniques remain old. For example, Bihar has 17 tractors per 1000 hectares against Punjab's 68 tractors per 1000 hectares.
- *Small, fragmented holdings:* Small and marginal farmers account for more than 90 per cent of all holdings. These small holdings work against economies of scale and deter the adoption of modern technology.
- *Diesel-based irrigation:* Irrigation is largely dependent on diesel-operated tube wells, the cost of running which has risen with recent increases in diesel prices.

Technology Transfer

- *Weak Agricultural Extension System:* The system for transfer of technology is very weak structurally in its capacity to absorb and disseminate modern technology. In fact, several extension systems exist simultaneously, and these need to be rationalized.
- *Flood and drought risks:* Recurrent floods in North Bihar districts and the paucity of rainfall in the South have hampered technology adoption.

Weak Marketing and Distribution Chain

- The lack of procurement has meant that farmers in Bihar often have to resort to distress sales in a season of plenty.
- *Inadequate storage and processing capacity:* An estimated 25 lakh MT storage capacity is required by the state, against an existing capacity of only 12 lakh MT. Proper storage infrastructure is also lacking at the primary level, and this has led to losses amounting at times to 50 per cent.

Agriculture is the mainstay of Bihar's economy, contributing 35 per cent to the state GDP and employing 77 per cent of the work force. The state has the ideal natural resources: fertile flat land, plenty of water, both surface and underground, and agro-climatic conditions suitable for cultivating a variety of crops to make agriculture its core competence. The mantra for the state can be stated in a few words: to maximize the use of vast untapped potential and natural endowments of the state, thereby ensuring food and nutritional security and better farm incomes, through environmentally sustainable agronomic practices.

Strategy for Major Food Grains

Rice

- Propagation of rice intensification (SRI) technology, hybrid varieties, *boro* rice supported by a strong seed programme, and fine and scented varieties to increase incomes.
- Replacement of long-duration varieties with short and medium duration varieties.

- Upgradation and strengthening of milling facilities, a strong procurement and NSP.
- In the terminal year of the Eleventh Plan, the targets for rice are as follows: Area—33.98 lakh hectares, Production—72.72 lakh MT, Productivity—21.43 quintal/hectare.

Maize

- Popularization of hybrid varieties supported by strong seed programme.
- Encouraging the cultivation of rabi maize, and baby corn, sweet corn and quality protein maize varieties for raising income, particularly in diara areas.
- Proper storage (including drying) and procurement and MSP.
- Promotion of a maize-based processing industry (animal feed, corn oil, starch, ethanol, etc.).
- Popularization of maize as food for people.
- In the terminal year of the Eleventh Plan, the targets for maize are as follows: Area—7.65 lakh hectares, Production—28.61 lakh MT, Productivity—37.41 quintal/hectare.

Wheat

- Timely sowing and harvesting.
- Development of short and medium duration varieties.
- Mechanization (combine harvesting and zero tillage sowing).
- In the terminal year of the Eleventh Plan, the targets for wheat are as follows: Area—20.85 lakh hectares, Production—48.06 lakh MT, Productivity—20.05 quintal/hectare.

Pulses

- Expansion of area (particularly of lentils, *moong*, and gram).
- Popularization of high yielding varieties supported by a strong seed programme.
- Rehabilitation of gram in agro-climatic zone I after the harvest of medium and late rice.

- Use of bio-fertilizer including Rhizobium.
- Improvement in farm drainage to reduce water logging.
- In the terminal year of the Eleventh Plan, the targets for pulses are as follows: Area—8.50 lakh hectares, Production—10.12 lakh MT, Productivity—11.94 quintal/hectare.

Oilseeds

- Area expansion.
- Replacing lathyrus and low yielding wheat with *rai*, *sarson*, sunflower.
- Popularization of high yielding varieties supported by a strong seed programme.
- Popularization of *paira* and intercropping of mustard.
- Use of sulphureous fertilizers.

In the terminal year of the Eleventh Plan, the targets for oilseeds are as follows: Area—1.77 lakh hectares, Production—1.73 lakh MT, Productivity—9.76 quintal/hectare.

Fruits and Vegetables

- Rejuvenation of old orchards.
- Area expansion.
- Assured supply of quality planting material.
- High density planting.
- Irrigation and drip and micro-sprinkler.
- Mechanization of harvesting, grading and packing.
- Processing and cold chain.
- In the terminal year of the Eleventh Plan, the targets for fruits and vegetables are as follows: Area—6.75 lakh hectares, Production—112.65 lakh MT, Productivity—16.70 quintal/hectare.

Agriculture: Action Points

- Increase crop productivity.

- Promote crop diversification through increased maize production and the promotion of fruit and vegetable cultivation.
- Improve technology transfer by strengthening the agricultural extension system to improve the quality and timeliness of inputs supply.
- Improve education and research into state-specific issues and varieties.
- Strengthen the existing marketing, processing and distribution chain.
- Promote micro-irrigation programmes to enhance water use efficiency.

Animal Husbandry

Animal husbandry and its allied activities, such as poultry farming, fisheries and so on, if developed appropriately, have the potential to significantly enhance the rural economy. Even at the present slow pace of development and underutilization, animal husbandry contributes 16 per cent to the GSDP (despite its low share of 0.75 per cent of total state budgetary allocation), a situation which is mirrored in the fisheries and dairy sectors. Despite this contribution the state is still not self-sufficient in milk, meat, eggs and fish production. These sectors have the capacity to provide opportunities for livelihood to people at the place where and in the situation in which they presently reside.

Bihar has abundant water resources such as ponds and tanks (covering approximately 65000 hectares) and major flowing rivers (around 2700 km in length), which are fertile breeding grounds for pisciculture. North Bihar also has captive fisheries resources like *chaurs* (low lying depressions filled with water) and ox-bow lakes. Converting these capture fisheries to culture fisheries could make them important sources of income and employment for the fishing communities, apart from being an excellent source of cheap protein for people.

Vision for the Eleventh Plan

Given the potential these sectors have to impact on rural poverty, incomes and livelihoods, animal husbandry, fisheries and the dairy sector will be promoted so that the state becomes self sufficient in these products. As major inputs for agro-processing, dairy and fisheries produce can become an important source for value addition within the state itself, which in turn opens up income and employment opportunities.

Fisheries

Bihar is one of the few states with large inland fisheries and aquaculture resources. The paradox of fisheries development in Bihar is that while it has large, untapped water resources for aquaculture, it depends on states like Andhra Pradesh for the supply of about half of its annual fish demand. The annual consumption of fish within the state is nearly 4.5 lakh tonnes, against the present annual production of around 2.25—2.50 lakh tonnes. The underutilization of aquaculture resources, unscientific management of water bodies and lack of entrepreneurship are some of the most obvious reasons for the gap between demand and supply. The major challenge, therefore, is to develop aquaculture resources for productive, sustainable fisheries to meet the local demand and enhance the nutritive and livelihood security to farmers as well as consumers.

Approach in the Eleventh Plan

The goal for fisheries development during the Eleventh Plan is for the state to expand production and increase productivity to national levels through the development of ponds and adoption of technically sound pisciculture practices. In addition, the establishment of hygienic storage conditions, rapid transportation systems and an efficient marketing network for fish will also help to increase socio-economic security in fishing communities.

For fish production to reach self-sufficiency levels, annual production levels would need to rise from the current 2.8 lakh tonnes to about 6 lakh tonnes. These calculations are based upon the average annual growth rate of 4 per cent in the fishery sector at the national level which could easily be increased to 10 per cent and 15 per cent in Bihar, because vertical and horizontal expansion of aquaculture is possible in the state.

Strategy for the Eleventh Plan

Output will be expanded through the creation of new water areas and renovation of the old ones, by bringing open water areas like ox-bow lakes, chaurs and command area flood plains under culture-based fisheries, and renovating ponds to increase cultivable water areas.

The quality of output will be upgraded by providing regular training to fisher folk, supplying quality fish seeds, setting up private and government carp-seed hatcheries, gradual and scientific conversion of capture fisheries resources into culture fisheries resources. National welfare programmes will be introduced to improve the livelihoods of the fishing communities.

Culture Fisheries

The major portion of fish production in Bihar is from ponds and tanks, but the share of culture fisheries in gross fish production can be increased threefold. Only 30 per cent of the ponds and tanks are scientifically managed, the rest need renovation and deepening. Farmers will need to be given proper technical training and incentives for composite fish culture. Private ponds and tanks will be developed through the cluster approach through bank financing coupled with subsidies. Funding from centrally sponsored schemes like NREGP (National Rural Employment Guarantee Programme) for the renovation of government tanks will need to be increased.

Capture Fisheries

With improved management, catches from open water bodies in Bihar can increase manifold, as can overall sustainability and the quality of output. More than one lakh hectares of water area are still untapped, used only to catch fish which have entered the waters during floods. If open water fishery is to remain a major contributor to overall inland fish production, some parallel processes to intensify yield have to be instituted. Several new techniques have been developed which could be appropriate for application in these areas. With this, output per hectare annually should rise to 600 kg of fish. The proposed Eleventh Plan targets of fisheries are at Table 1.9.

Table 1.9: Fisheries: Proposed Eleventh Plan Targets

Growth Indicators Physical Targets	*2007-08*	*2008-09*	*2009-10*	*2010-11*	*2011-12*
Fish production (lakh metric tonnes)	340	350	360	370	380
Fish seed production (million)	450	470	490	520	550
Farmers' training (number)	4000	4000	4000	4000	4000
Housing and other civic amenities for fisher folk (number)	400	400	400	400	400
Construction of seed hatcheries (number)	4	4	4	4	4

ANIMAL HUSBANDRY: ACTION POINTS

Animal Husbandry

- Improve the health of livestock by:
  - Establishing 1000 new veterinary hospitals,
  - Modernizing and strengthening the Institute of Animal Health and Production in Patna,
  - Establishing a veterinary public health service to regulate and monitor various functions,
  - Establishing the newly constituted Bihar Livestock Development Agency, and
  - Enhancing the skills of government veterinarians.
- Improve the stock of small ruminants (sheep and goats).
- Promote backyard poultry, piggery and small dairy units.
- Establish infrastructure for mastitis control and training.

Dairy

- Increase milk production:
  - Through improved breeds, proper health-care and management of milch animals,
  - Building skills of milk producers in proper feeding methods and better management of stock.
- Strengthen milk cooperatives and increase mopping up of surplus milk.

- Popularize clean milk production.
- Expand the coverage of milk cooperatives to include more areas and villages.
- Create additional processing capacities by expanding existing plants and setting up new ones.
- Promote production with Total Quality Management, ISO and HACCP certification and better dairy plant management for cost control.
- Enhance capacities of enriched feed production plants.

Fisheries

- Restore and renovate traditional water bodies,
- Popularize fish seed production (the state produces only half of its fish seed requirement),
- Bring ox-bow lakes under culture-based fisheries,
- Develop water logged areas into aquaculture estates,
- Optimize fish yield from reservoirs,
- Popularize integrated fish farming,
- Establish a network that links farms to retail outlets, and
- Provide insurance coverage for houses, drinking water, community centres, health and family welfare facility for fish farmers.

Water Management and Irrigation

Vision for the Eleventh Plan

Irrigation is a key enabler for agriculture-based growth. Through improved technical, financial and economic use of water resources, the sector's contribution to the agriculture development plan would be crucial. Other objectives will be to enhance sustainability of growth through proper management and upkeep of water resources systems, improve equity through better targeting of development programmes to the rural poor, and increased use of IT for real time monitoring for flood forecasting and in managing overall water resources.

Strategy

Achieving the growth rate proposed for the Eleventh Plan will require the creation of 13.86 lakh hectares of additional potential (Table 1.10).

Table 1.10: Irrigation: Additional Potential during the Eleventh Plan

(lakh hectares)

Schemes	*Creation of Additional Irrigation Potential*	*Restoration of Lost Irrigation Potential*
On-going schemes	3.19	—
ERM schemes	—	1.87
New schemes	8.80	—
Grant Total	13.86 lakh hectares	

There will be an emphasis on rainwater harvesting and propagating rainfed agriculture, especially as large areas in South Bihar are devoid of assured irrigation due to various factors. There is increasing acceptance that proper maintenance of conveyance requires management by the beneficiaries. The State Government has made significant progress in this area by transferring the operation, maintenance and upkeep of 32 distributaries aggregating a total command of 110549 hectares to Water Users Associations (WUAs) (Table 1.11).

Table 1.11: Progress on Transfer of Maintenance to WUAs

Number of systems transferred to WUA	32
Number of farmers' societies registered	07
Number of societies which have applied for registration	38
Number of societies whose applications are being formalized	15
Number of societies in the process of being formed	518
Total	610

Minor Irrigation

Minor irrigation includes all irrigation schemes, surface and groundwater, covering a cultivable command area upto 2000 hectares, and include minor surface water-flow irrigation schemes, surface water-lift irrigation schemes, and groundwater utilization schemes, through open wells, shallow tube wells and deep tube wells.

Strategy for the Eleventh Plan

To meet the irrigation needs of the State, the strategy during the Eleventh Plan will be the speedy development of potential, improving the utilization of the developed potential, expanding irrigation benefits to unirrigated land, increasing the supply of private electric-based tube wells, increasing subsidies for wells and pumps; and increasing sustainability by strengthening water users' associations.

SURFACE IRRIGATION: CREATING AND RESTORING IRRIGATION POTENTIAL

About 165000 hectares of additional potential will be created and 400000 hectares of lost potential restored through surface irrigation schemes mainly through restoration and renovation of *Ahars* and *Pynes* (traditional water bodies).

- The State Government will add minor irrigation potential of 80000 hectares by completing surface schemes under RIDF, through the repair, renovation and restoration of water bodies under the Bharat Nirman Programme for the first two years of the Eleventh Plan. The same rate of creation of additional minor irrigation potential will be maintained for the last three years of the Plan by creating additional 85000 hectares of potential under these schemes.
- The State Government will also undertake the repair, renovation and restoration of traditional water bodies like *Ahars* and *Pynes*. Under the RSVY, about 8000 *Ahars* and *Pynes* will be repaired and renovated, which will restore about 400000 hectares of lost potential. Other schemes under RIDF will include weir, sluice gates and check dams on small streams and rivers.

Groundwater Resources

The ultimate potential of annually replenishable ground water resources reserved for irrigation is 48.57 lakh hectares. Potential of about 30 lakh hectares will be created by 2006-07. This leaves about 18.57 lakh hectares of unexploited irrigation potential from ground water to be developed during the Eleventh Plan. There is no immediate threat of over-exploitation of ground water resources as ground water depletion is on average 50 to 55 per cent of the annual replenishable resources.

About 14.4 lakh hectares of additional irrigation potential can be created by exploiting the ground water resources through various schemes: extending the private shallow tube well programme under the RSVY; schemes to build 3000 medium duty deep tube wells under the NABARD's RIDF Phase-XI and 6000 medium duty deep tube wells under RIDF subsequent phases. About 2.10 lakh hectare of lost potential of the state tube wells will be restored by renovation of 45000 old state tube wells which have completed their useful life for which a scheme will be posed to NABARD under RIDF phase XII.

The life of ground water irrigation structure like tube wells and pump sets is approximately 20 years, so on average 5 per cent of ground water structures go out of service every year. To maintain the level of created potential, about 25000 shallow private tube wells and 1000 state deep tube wells need to be replaced every year beyond the Tenth Plan period.

Table 1.12: Depicts the Minor Irrigation Potential Created/Utilized till 2005-06

Minor Irrigation Potential in Bihar	*Area (lakh hectares)*
Surface schemes including traditional *ahar* and *pynes*	15.44
Ground water utilization schemes of open wells, shallow tube wells, deep tube wells	48.57
Total	*64.01*
Minor irrigation potential created	
Ground water schemes	28.99
Surface water schemes	7.27
Total	*36.26*
Irrigation potential utilized in 2005-06	
Surface water including lift and barge schemes	0.49
Surface water *ahar*, *pynes* and traditional systems	3.32
State tube wells	0.25
Private tube wells and irrigation wells	27.64
Total	*31.70*

Irrigation: Action Points

- Create irrigation potential in 22.15 lakh hectares.
- Restore *ahars* and *pynes*.

- Restore state tube well and lift irrigation schemes.
- Incentives execution of private shallow tube well schemes, including replacement of old tube wells.
- Monitor project outcomes rather than outlays.
- Propagate rainfed agriculture, giving priority to rain water harvesting; and ground water recharge.
- Capacity building for WUAs (Water Users Associations)—essential social factors to be looked into.

Rural Development

Bihar, the biggest challenge as India's third most populous state, is eliminating poverty, especially in the rural areas. The vast majority (90%) of Bihar's population lives in villages, and 44.3 per cent of the rural population lives below the poverty line (BPL). This corresponds to a current population of 3.6 crore, or 80-90 lakh families. A recent household survey conducted by the State Government indicates that this figure of rural population below the poverty line may be even large. This indication requires redoubling our efforts to achieve much higher growth rates and reorienting our strategy to reduce the number of people living below the poverty line. Bihar's land area is 3 per cent of India's, it supports 10 per cent of India's rural BPL families; 34.3 lakh families are still shelterless (Table 1.13). Bihar also has the highest net migration rates among all states with 0.39 males and 0.17 females per 100 population.

Bihar has no significant rural development plan schemes of its own and depends heavily on centrally financed schemes which provide significant additions to its resources for anti-poverty programmes. The current National Rural Employment Guarantee Scheme (Sampoorna Grameen Rozgar Yojana, Swarnajayanti Gram Swarozgar Yojana, Indira Awas Yojana and Hariyali) address the basic requirements of wage employment, livelihoods, shelter and improving the productive capacity of land. Since the NREGS was notified to cover only 23 out of 38 districts, the Bihar government covered the remaining 15 districts under an identical scheme named the State REGS. However, the implementation of all rural development schemes needs substantial improvement to achieve the desired outcomes.

Table 1.13: Demographics and the Rural Economy

	India	*Bihar*	*Bihar's Share in the National %*
Total 2001 population (crores)	102.86	8.30	8.1
Rural 2001 population (crores)	74.25	7.43	10.1
Rural population (%)	72.1	89.5	
Area (000 sq. km)	3287	94	2.9
Population density/sq. km	313	881	
Population growth rate (%)	1.6	1.8	
BPL (% 1999-2000)	26.1	42.6	
Rural BPL (%)	27.1	44.3	
Rural BPL population (crores)	20.12	3.29	16.4
Projected rural BPL population (for 2006 in lakhs)	21.78	3.60	
No. of BPL families 2006 (lakhs)	545	90	
Projected total population in 2015 (crores)	125.40	10.27	8.2
Projected rural population in 2015 (crores)	86.63	9.19	10.6
MDG target BPL families (lakhs)	12.26	2.02	
Target No. of BPL families (lakhs)	282	50.50	
Poverty growth elasticity	-0.73	-0.43	
Shelterless families (lakhs)		42.1	

Eleventh Plan Goals

Bihar's vision is to become a developed state by 2015, which requires a rapid reduction in poverty. The first Millennium Development Goal is to halve, between 1990 and 2015, the proportion of people whose income is less than $1 a day and the proportion of people who suffer from hunger. For Bihar, this means reducing the BPL population to 22 per cent by 2015 or by about 1.5 per cent per year. Achieving the poverty related MDG would therefore depend heavily on rapid growth in the non-farm activities because, till now, growth in agriculture with relatively low productivity has had a limited impact on poverty.

In addition, to increase the productive capacity of Bihar's vast young population, major efforts will be required in education, health and skills development, especially in the rural areas to equip future generations to engage in productive, gainful occupations. This will also serve to stem the out-migration from the state.

Education and skill development largely benefit those below 20 years of age, i.e. the next generation. The hunger and poverty of those above 20 would have to be tackled by direct measures to provide the basic minimum needs of *roti*, *kapda*, *makan*, *bijli*, *sadak*, and *pani*, and even broadband, with an emphasis on women's empowerment.

This can be achieved by guaranteed wage employment, productive livelihood through self-employment, and providing houses for the rural poor. In addition, appropriate land and water development programmes can strengthen the rural economy and improve rural livelihoods.

Eleventh Plan Strategy

Poverty can be reduced more effectively not only through programmes targeting the poor but through inclusive growth with a shift in employment to non-farm activities. This calls for an integrated strategy covering human resource development through improved access to education, health, drinking water, sanitation, welfare and labour, and economic development through increased opportunities in industry, agriculture, animal husbandry, irrigation, energy, transport and telecom, supplemented with targeted programmes for the poor, especially women. Increasingly, powers to deal with these subjects are devolving upon Panchayati Raj Institutions which will have a major role in improving governance. With 38 Zila Parishads, 534 Panchayat Samitis and 8463 Gram Panchayats, quick communication and transparency are essential for these Panchayat Institutions to be effective. Fortunately, in today's inter-connected world, technology provides a solution through broadband Internet.

The basic minimum needs of *Roti*, *Kapda*, *Makan*, can be met through wage employment, self-employment and rural housing. Therefore, the existing rural employment guarantee and watershed development schemes, Swarnajayanti Gram Swarozgar Yojana and Indira Awas Yojana would continue as thrust programmes for the elimination of hunger and deprivation.

Increasing Farm and Non-Farm Productivity

The poverty-related MDG of halving the BPL percentage by 2015 corresponds to a target of reducing the rural BPL percentage from 44 per cent in 2000 to 22 per cent in 2015. This means that about 50 lakh rural families will need to be raised above the poverty line by

2015, i.e. about 16.7 lakh families during the Eleventh Plan, or 3.3 lakh rural families per year.

Assuming the elasticity of 0.4 between growth in GDP and fall in the BPL percentage, the target of 1.5 per cent reduction per year in rural BPL population requires a GDP growth of about 4 per cent per year. The growth rate of agriculture is well below this. Thus, efforts will necessarily have to aim at faster non-farm sector growth along with strategies to rapidly increase agricultural productivity by focusing on horticulture, applying most recent remunerative techniques such as vermiculture, non-chemical pest management and other productivity-boosting practices, many of which are labour intensive.

Rural Development: Action Points

- Meet basic minimum needs through wage-employment, self-employment and rural housing,
- Revise programme guidelines to emphasize women's empowerment, through a processes and outcomes approach,
- Restore the delivery capability of the field machinery through intensive capacity building,
- Encourage the formation of active Panchayati Raj Institutions and Civil Society Organizations to empower the people,
- Implement effectively the Right to Information Act and IT enabled systems,
- Outsource IT functions through PPP, and
- Promote technology appropriate for rural conditions.

Elementary Education

The state has taken an unprecedented decision to appoint 2.36 lakh elementary and secondary school teachers to clear the entire backlog of vacancies and bring all out-of-school children into the elementary school. The salient features of this mega teacher recruitment process are as follows:

- The policy decision is specifically aimed at bringing teacher-pupil ratio to the national norm of 1 : 40.

- Teacher's positions (60000) have been created for schooling 24 lakh out-of-school children, largely employed as domestic servants, in *dhabas*, hotels, restaurants, etc.
- The system of para-teachers or contract teachers has been abolished to secure equality and social justice in the school system.
- The recruitment has been decentralized and is being done by the Panchayati Raj Institutions (PRIs).
- Because of gradual shift to the PRIs and with a combination of liberal service conditions, the new recruits are being offered consolidated salaries to enable the state government for huge expansion in the teaching force.

In addition to teacher, 15000 new schools are being opened after abolishing around 14000 learning or EGS centres. The concept of building a 'school' and not adding classrooms as under the SSA has been introduced and the programme of 'Mukhya Mantri Samagra Vidyalaya Vikas' has been launched. For this programme, the state has provided funds from its budget for major repairs and improvements of school buildings, facilities for games and sports and construction of boundary walls. Provisions for toilets, drinking water, kitchen sheds, etc. are being converged under schemes of different departments. This is yet another scheme for addressing the question of equality and social justice in the school system.

Drop-out has been a major challenge at the national level, and Bihar is no exception to it. In Bihar, dropouts have been largely due to the absence of adequate number of schools and teachers for over a decade or so. Wherever schools were available, teachers were engaged in several non-teaching activities, or were dragged into courts for service related matters. These factors are being addressed and will continue to be done during the Eleventh Plan. In addition, the government plans to launch a scheme of 'conditional cash transfer' to parents, which will be used for purchasing school uniforms for all children upto grade V, and for all girls up to grade VIII. This scheme should reduce dropouts particularly of girls at the upper primary level. While the state government will be able to mobilize resources this year, it will need central assistance for sustaining it during the Eleventh Plan.

SUMMING UP: BIHAR

Work culture in Bihar needs a radical overhaul; the increasing pace of development calls for fast communication with field officers, and technological cost-effective solutions need to be implemented. The Eleventh Plan proposes to strengthen service delivery through a multidimensional approach. Administrative reforms have been initiated and will be followed up to build capacity and strengthen institutions for skill upgradation, which will equip projects to avail funds from the Central Government and other sources. At the same time, the effectiveness of the service delivery systems will need to be improved by preventing leakages and improving expenditure efficiency. The approach targets an overall improvement in education and health outcomes through combined inputs from private, public and non-governmental organizations. This is especially important in rural areas where the quality and access to services have been weakest and the indicators poorest.

The Role of Local Bodies

An important dimension of the approach to improving public administration and governance in the Eleventh Plan will be increased accountability both at the level of the state and within sectoral service delivery units. The lack of public accountability has increased corruption. Inclusive growth will call for the government to become more accountable to the people by strengthening institutions that enforce accountability such as local bodies.

People's participation in programmes through community-based organizations and Panchayati Raj Institutions is thus extremely necessary for ensuring accountability. One way is to devolve responsibilities to local government bodies that can plan and implement programme with the participation of civil society. PRIs will play a definitive role in the formulation and implementation of the Eleventh Plan objectives. The state has already made progress in devolution to the third tier as Panchayati Raj Institutions (PRI) elections have been held; against 50 per cent reservation for women, 58 per cent were actually elected.

Bihar's extensive network of women's self-help groups is another avenue for collaboration. Using such resources to further effective service delivery will also empower local people.

Improved Programme Implementation

One lesson that has been repeatedly emphasized but not applied in the implementation of these programmes is that rural development is essentially process-oriented and not a target-driven system. Programme guidelines need to be revised to emphasize an orientation towards processes and outcomes, rather than targets.

The efficacy of the Eleventh Plan strategy would depend critically on the implementation machinery. The delivery capability of field administration needs to be built up in different ways, including intensive capacity-building. Training should focus on ways to secure and increase people's involvement, participatory rural appraisal, human resource management, accounts, information technology and project management, through exposure to other states and best practices.

Large numbers of technical and functional vacancies need to be filled and minimum tenures ensured both in the secretariat and field postings. Recruitment, capacity building and empowerment will take time, and in the meanwhile, several functions can be outsourced on a PPP basis.

Bihar: Overall Action Points

- Focus on improving physical infrastructure especially in key sectors such as agriculture and industry.
- Focus on increasing productivity in agriculture and allied sectors through better implementation of schemes, by building related infrastructure, and strengthening marketing and distribution networks.
- Undertake fiscal reforms to mobilize public resources and savings vital to finance the state's ambitious development strategy.
- Undertake administrative reforms, capacity building and institutional strengthening to improve delivery of services to the poor.
- Improve governance through increased transparency, instituting the Right to Information, and more intensive use of information technology to increase the participation of

citizens and non-governmental organizations in developmental programmes.

- Strengthen programmes and schemes by monitoring outcomes rather than outlays.
- Adopt a multi-dimensional approach to improving educational and health outcomes with participation from private, public and non-governmental organizations.
- Increase community participation in service delivery by promoting PRIs and women's SHGs.
- Facilitate an enhanced role for private investment in key areas such as power, agri-business, technical training and educational institutes, ancillary health services, etc.

2

West Bengal

M.N. ROY

West Bengal has made sustained efforts to reach the benefits of development to all sections of the people particularly those belonging to the vulnerable groups. Land Reforms, Decentralized Planning, setting up of Self Help Groups on a wide scale, Mass Literacy and 'Health for All' programmes are the major policy initiatives that have substantially benefited wide cross-sections of people of the state. It is worthwhile to mention that land reforms measures, institutional framework in the form of PRIs, decentralized planning process, empowerment of the people with focus on women accompanied by synergy in the activities of different departments have been the major contributory factors to the healthy growth of the state's economy. It has achieved an average annual growth rate of 7.5 per cent in its SDP (at constant prices) during the 10th Plan period, with the annual rate of growth showing a rising trend in the last two years, with 8.07 per cent in 2005-06 and 8.20 per cent in 2006-07. Its per capita income also increased at an average annual rate of 5.47 per cent in this period. This growth in income in the 10th Plan has also been accompanied by improving health status of the population in the state as is evident in the significant decline in the birth rate, death rate and infant mortality rate at the end of 2005. According to the state-wise data published by the Government of India (2005), the death rate in this state has fallen to 0.6 per thousand, which is not only lower than the All India average (7.4), but also the lowest, along with Kerala, among all the states. The infant mortality rate in this state has now fallen to 38, which is again much lower than the All India average (59) and the fourth among the states, after Kerala (14), Maharashtra (36) and

Tamil Nadu (37). The birth rate in urban areas has also fallen to 12.6 which is lowest among the urban areas of all the states. Literacy in the state during the 10th Plan has also improved. According to the NSS 60th Round Report on Household Consumer Expenditure (January-June, 2004), overall literacy has increased to 72.2 per cent in 2004 from 68.64 per cent in 2001. In the health and education sectors not only have their outcome indicators improved during the 10th Plan, but also in both these sectors considerable progress has been made in improving and expanding the physical infrastructure as well as the quality of the available service. The SDP (at constant prices) from agriculture in West Bengal over the period from 1993-94 to 2003-04 has grown at an average annual rate of 3.64 per cent, which is not only much higher than the average annual rate of growth (1.53%) of SDP from agriculture for all the states over the same period, but is also the highest among all the states (*Source*: Central Statistical Organization, Government of India). For the remaining three years of the 10th Plan period, 2004-05 to 2006-07, the average annual rate of growth of SDP from agriculture has been 2.50 per cent, which would have been much higher but for the widespread floods affecting the agricultural production in each of these years. Moreover, according to the NSS 55th Round (1999-2000) 46.62 of the total workforce in the state was employed in the agricultural sector (inclusive of agriculture, animal husbandry, fishery and forestry sectors). In 2004-05 (NSS 61st Round) the agriculture sector employed 45.78 per cent of the total workforce in the state. Thus, the share of the agriculture sector in the total workforce has declined only marginally during this period. On the other hand, as is usual, the share of the agriculture sector (as defined above) in total SDP (at constant 1999-2000 prices) has declined progressively from 30.86 per cent in 2001-02 to 28.60 per cent in 2003-04 and to 27.17 per cent in 2004-05 as a result of the impact of the differential sectoral growth rates. This implies that 45.78 per cent of the state's workforce produced only 27.17 per cent of the total state income. This relative overcrowding of the agriculture sector inhibits the intensification of the production process.

Despite this growth in agriculture, there is a significant scope for improving the hectare yield of crops as well as increasing the cropping intensity through wider extension of irrigation facilities and adoption of comprehensive drainage and flood-protection schemes.

The growth in employment in the rural and urban areas of the state between 1999-2000 and 2004-05 (NSS 55th and 61st Rounds) has been 3.34 per cent and 3.56 per cent per annum, respectively. These growth rates were higher than the annual rate of growth of the labour force during this period. Moreover, combined (rural + urban) poverty (per cent below the poverty line) has declined from 27.02 per cent in 1999-2000 (NSS 55th Round) to 20.60 per cent in 2004-05 (NSS 61st Round).

The industry sector in the state, which was dominated by the traditional labour intensive industries at the beginning of the 9th Plan, faced adverse situation because of the telling effect of the New Economic Policy (NEP) introduced by the Central Government in 1991. In fact, the new policy regime exposed this sector to uneven competition particularly from the products coming to the Indian market in the prevailing Free Trade Regime. Although a large number of new capital-intensive units were set up in the state especially from the late nineties, the production of these new units could commence only after a gestation lag. This new phase of the industrial development, i.e. the gradual decline of the old traditional industries and coming on stream of new productive units with a lag, therefore, had a regressive effect on the movement of industrial production in the state. However, in the 10th Plan period, the average rate of growth of SDP from organized and unorganized manufacturing sector was 7.4 per cent. In 2005-07, this rate of growth has been 8.8 per cent which clearly indicates that the state has been able to effectively counter the situation and face the challenges of the unfolding realities. This has been possible because of the enabling situation created by the state government for more and more investment through a set of measures and policy initiatives appropriate to the demand of the ground realities.

Most other indicators of social and economic development have also been satisfactory during the 10th Plan. Especially significant has been the average annual growth rate of 8.1 per cent of the tertiary sector during the first three years of the 10th Plan.

While the sectoral performance of the economy has been according to expectations during the 10th Plan, further improvement in future will, however, be dependent on macro-economic stability in the country. Integral to this also is the state's ability to garner adequate resources for increasing public investment during the 11th Plan not only for sustaining the investment demand in the economy but also to ensure an inclusive growth process. The West Bengal economy registered an average annual growth rate of 7.11 per cent in its SDP (at constant prices) between 1994-95 and 2001-02. Its per capita income increased at an average annual rate of 5.51 per cent in the same period. In the 10th Plan (first three years) West Bengal continued to post 'over 7 per cent' growth in its SDP and 'over 5 per cent' growth of its per capita income.

These growth rates could be achieved when the state was facing severe fiscal crises especially in the later years of the 9th Plan and during the 10th Plan period. Moreover, it is expected that there will be significant improvement of performance in the agriculture and allied sectors in the 11th Plan period. It is also expected that the manufacturing sector will register a growth of 10 per cent. It will be the state's endeavour to increase the growth from the agriculture sector to 4 per cent per annum. As the production structure in agriculture is broad-based, such a growth will have significant impact on the quality of life in the rural areas and could, through generation of off-the-farm activities, reduce the dependence on cultivation.

Thus an annual growth rate of the State Domestic Product (at constant prices) ranging from 9 per cent will be the target for the 11th Plan.

The state, in keeping with the basic objective of increasing the scope of livelihood of the masses, has carried out land reforms and provided crucial non-land inputs to the beneficiaries of the land reform measures so as to allow them to take up productive activities. In other sectors also the state's policy has been to encourage and facilitate the economic activities of the small producers. These policies together with the intensification of the panchayat based decentralized planning process have directed the growth of the economy towards benefiting every section of the society.

However, in recent years it has been experienced that it is becoming increasingly difficult to sustain such a small producer-centric economic system because of the competition from larger economic entities following the liberalization of the Indian economy. While some of these emerging trends have far reaching consequences it remains a fact that over the past two decades and a half the ability of the state to bring large segments of the rural and urban poor into the productive fold has created the demand base for a sustained growth of the state's economy. The growth in agricultural production, rapid increase in small scale and unorganized manufacturing units specially in the rural areas as well as growth in the service sector and the consistently high growth in per capita income, together with the rapid improvement of the health indicators and the reduction of rural and urban poverty (which was around 50 per cent in the mid-seventies) have proved the efficacy and effectiveness of the strategy. It is, therefore, the policy of the State Government to pursue this basic strategy and to synchronize it with the unfolding realities both at the national and global levels. However, within the broad ambit of this small producer centric strategy, newly emerging problems as in the agricultural sector during the 10th Plan, will be addressed through a judicious mix of government intervention and market trends.

In West Bengal, the size of population and its density are high in proportion to available land having serious implications for sustainable quality of life overtime. Efforts would be made to ensure that runway population situation does not overtake plan initiatives in the state. Demographically explosive zones would be monitored through programme efforts by means of transparent monitoring format.

The main focus of the 11th Plan is sustainable development through the route of integrated development strategy where the qualitative improvement of the life of the people at different rungs of the society is the basic intention. Empowerment of the people, infrastructure development, intensification of mass literacy programme, creation of world class health facilities, agricultural growth, rapid industrialization, reducing regional imbalances, bridging the urban-rural gaps, strengthening of the SHGs, good governance, institution-building ensuring people's access to opportunities and development of scientific temperament among the people will be the guiding principles in pursuing this strategy. The targeted reduction in poverty would be attained through higher growth of income from the agriculture sector (inclusive of animal husbandry, fishery and forest sectors). This, supplemented by rapid growth of the non-farm sector in the rural areas, increasing government expenditure on rural poverty, employment and infrastructure development programmes, intensification of SHG network for generating self-employment, private sector investment in the post-harvest infrastructure of the horticulture and other sectors like animal husbandry, fisheries, etc. is expected to significantly impact on the quality of life of the people of the rural area. This process of rising production and investment would be complemented by the provision of supplementary nutrition to children and pregnant and lactating mothers, strengthening of the public distribution system, providing improved health care facilities, ensuring rapid spread of literacy and scope for technical and vocational training, providing safe drinking water and ensuring general improvement in hygiene in rural households, etc.

Incidentally, the Self Help Groups scheme as a supporting programme initiative has been taken up in the state as a component to enlarge poverty alleviation programme as well as the social sector programme for the poorest of the poor women groups. This labour intensive initiative based on principles of equity and social justice is likely to ensure that women programme partners actually reap the benefits of the economic and social programmes. SHGs have become programme partners of various schemes administered by plan implementing departments and also the bank linked programme of the NABARD. The social intermediation programmes followed by the NGOs have accelerated the process of organizing the poor particularly women into Self Help Groups. More than 100000 Self Help Groups have been formed by different organizations with Swarna Jayanti Gram Swarojgar Yojana (SGSY) contributing around 55699 SHGs. Self Help Groups are partners for about 20 programmes being implemented in the state. However, the optimum use of them has still to take a definite pattern and the specific assessment of employment potential and the location specific requirement of SHGs network have to be worked out. For programme convergence of SHGs based programme at the grassroots level the necessity of the formation of a Federation of SHGs has been felt. 15 blocks in five districts have been selected for the experimentation of this project.

The size of credit and the need for its linkage are crucial factors requiring SHG growth with professional mode. The need for training for exposure to market behaviour and for utilizing market related facilities need to be professionally dealt with.

In areas where extreme poverty grips the people, convergence of programmes of different departments will be ensured. Thus, programmes of the Rural Development, Women and Child Development, Food and Civil Supplies, PHE, Health, etc. will be targeted specially to these areas. The coverage of supplementary nutrition programme will be intensified. Above all, the scope for income generating activities will be enlarged through the creation of irrigation facilities, supply of inputs and credit, formation of SHGs, etc. Similar efforts will be made in pockets with high concentration of the disadvantaged sections of the rural population, which might not be coterminous with the above areas. In other words, all efforts will be converged for a qualitative improvement of the life of the people who live on the margin. In the 11th Plan efforts will be made to improve the quality of employment. In order to achieve this, attempts will be made to draw investment in small and medium enterprises (SME), IT and related service sectors, real estate and building industry, organized tertiary sectors, etc. The rapid growth of these major sectors would induce the growth of the unorganized and informal sector. The envisaged large investment on urban renewal projects and on green-field urban projects would also generate considerable employment during the 11th Plan. The scope of self-employment programmes will be enlarged further. Moreover, in order to continue with the 'all inclusive' growth process, the small producer centric production structure will be promoted across all sectors during the 11th Plan. It is envisaged that with the declining urban 'income poverty', easy availability of quality health services, spread of literacy, removing of the residual illiteracy in urban areas, health and education inadequacies in urban areas will be considerably 'reduced at the end of the 11th Plan'.

The state is now on a steady integration mode between vibrant agricultural economy and the emerging sectors of modern industrial economy. As has already been stated at the outset, the state has to navigate through uneven contours for the realization of its own vision mainly because of the Constitutional limitation that allows little scope to the State Government to pursue industrial policy independent of the one followed at the central level. With the process of globalization and liberalization gathering momentum and the old traditional labour intensive industries declining and the cottage and small scale sector facing stiff competition in the globalized economic scenario, the task of accelerating the process of industrial development of the state on the basis of the felt needs of the people is faced with new challenges with far reaching socio-political implications. It needs to be emphasized that though the service sector has been registering steady growth accompanied by new employment opportunities, the halting growth of the manufacturing sector has impacted on the employment scenario as a whole. Though the IT and ITES sectors have created substantial employment opportunities for the urban youth, steady growth of the manufacturing sector is crucial to the overall improvement of employment scenario. It is also equally important to ensure the steady growth of the cottage and small scale industries to further improve the situation. The State Government will make vigorous efforts in the 11th Plan to address the issue of unemployment both in the rural and urban areas. The agriculture production structure will increasingly come under the threat of cheap imports and supply of agricultural products from other states. Moreover, rising cost and almost stagnant harvest prices have eroded the profitability of crop cultivation. In this situation, rising productivity could ensure competitiveness of the crops produced by farmers in the state.

In full appreciation of the ground realities particularly in the agriculture and allied sector, the State Government will adopt suitable strategy to ensure vibrant growth of the rural economy where the Panchayati Raj System will have a dominant role and the network of SHGs will be expanded further as a measure of empowerment of women as well as to involve them in economic activities by increasing their number. This is aimed at accelerating the process of socio-economic transformation of the state.

Another important area of intervention will be to increase public investment in the rural sector (specially in the cultivation related sectors). This will induce private investment in the agriculture sector. The growth of productivity in the agriculture sector is crucially dependent on this.

Finally, the 11th Five Year Plan of West Bengal would endeavour to secure visible outcomes of all programme initiatives. Ensuring outcomes of programme initiatives would be the central focus of monitoring for all sectors of the economy with special focus on livelihood issues and social sector related areas on education, health and drinking water, etc. Outcome monitoring for inclusive growth would also be institutionalized. This would be so focused by all the decentralized programme partners. In addition, in recent years there have been repeated floods adversely affecting vast cropped areas and thereby preventing what could have been a much higher growth in agricultural production. This calls for the introduction of comprehensive drainage and flood-protection schemes.

AGRICULTURE

Although the marginal fragmented holdings are in general unviable, ownership of land bestows a number of advantages to a rural household. It ensures greater availability of credit. It provides security in adversity. Farmers earn some income, however meagre, from these tiny plots. Moreover, West Bengal is a land scarce state. Intensive utilization of the land in the state is a must. Small farmers use the land more intensively than big farmers through higher cropping intensity. According to the NSS, 59th Round Report on Income, Expenditure and Productive Assets of Urban Households (2003), the highest record of production and employment generation per hectare is obtained from the lands of small and marginal farmers. It may also be noted from the NSS data (55th and 61st Rounds) that between 1999-2000 and 2004-05, the rate of growth of employment (Current Daily Status) in the rural areas of West Bengal has been 4.46 per cent which is much higher than the corresponding all India figure (2.86%).

An exercise carried out showed that with the rising yield rate and somewhat stagnant demand for the staple rice, a large cultivable area presently under rice could be released for other crops. Thus if the area is diverted to the horticulture crops and huge investments in infrastructure take place, the potential for rapid growth of the food processing sector would be created. This would create substantial employment opportunities in the rural areas and reduce the over-crowding in the agricultural sector. The expanding market opportunities nationally and globally will also be tapped to ensure steady growth of this sector.

Attempt will also be made to use the area released from the cultivation of the staple crop for animal husbandry (fodder cultivation). The rapid growth of the animal husbandry sector would also allow absorption of some of the farmers engaged in cultivation. The growth of this sector as well as that of the fishery sector will also be consolidated through the creation of sector specific infrastructure. The development of these sectors would also generate downstream processing units. Horticultural products, animal husbandry products and even fishery provide scope for value addition and, therefore, have multiplier effect on employment. In other words, serious efforts will be made to transform the agriculture to agri-business in the best interests of the farmers.

The growth of rural industries like handloom, sericulture and other unregistered manufacturing industries will also be paced up and integrated with the sectors integral to the overall growth of the rural economy.

The new entity of micro industries that provides scope for financial as well as other assistance to the large number of rural units in the manufacturing and service sectors will also be encouraged as part of developing the agriculture sector. In addition, attempt will be made to attract large-scale industrial investment during the 11th Plan, for having a compelling effect on absorbing some of those employed in the agriculture sector. In fine, a two-pronged strategy of rapid industrialization and the process of agricultural growth through increased productivity, diversification, modernization and agribusiness will be pursued to combat the problem of over-crowding in the agriculture sector.

The falling prices and rising cost of cultivation could impel the more dynamic of the cultivators to intensify the cultivation process through mechanization. They could also resort to leasing in more land. The process has already started in the state. Farmers mainly having 4 to 10 hectares of land are resorting to this. If the practice is emulated by the small and marginal farmers widely, it is likely to develop a new pattern in the agriculture sector. The State Government will consider intervening in this regard within the existing legal framework if situation so demands.

Despite the actual expenditure (CAG) data, showing that the plan expenditure of the State Government in agriculture and rural development has increased from Rs. 1899 crores in ten-year period from 1985-86 to 1994-95 by nearly 100 per cent to Rs. 3622 crores in the next ten-year period from 1995-96 to 2004-05, and that state's plan expenditure in irrigation and drainage has increased from Rs. 1122 crores in 1985-86 to 1994-95 by more than 100 per cent to Rs. 2601 crores in 1995-96 to 2004-05, there is a need for further enhancement of public expenditure in this sphere.

While these structural factors impede productivity enhancing activities by the cultivators, the stagnancy in the yield rates of most crops in the state in recent years is also related to the declining public sector investment in the agriculture sector. A large increase in public investment in the agriculture sector is, therefore, imperative to increase agricultural productivity and induce private investment.

Every effort will be made to increase the productivity of different crops. The distribution of improved variety of seeds of different crops will be ensured. The benefits from using these seeds, as well as from adapting improved farming techniques will be popularized among farmers through proper extension activities. Extension personnel will be properly trained so as to import the latest technical inputs to the farmers. Knowledge Centres will be set up at the Block and GP levels with agricultural graduates to provide technical assistance to the farmers at their farm gates. Infrastructures will be developed to percolate the benefits of scientific research and technological innovations to the farmers. Agro clinics will be organized and crop doctors will be pressed into service for providing training in improved practices from sowing to harvesting well as to motivate the farmers for correct choice of crops so as to increase the productivity of land to the benefit of small and marginal farmers. Field applications of biotechnology will be made after taking due care against intrusion of genetically modified crops. The Universities of the State where agricultural research occupies pride of place will be effectively utilized to achieve the desired objectives. Other requirements like irrigation, soil conservation, reclamation of wasteland, etc. that are necessary to increase the productivity of existing cultivable land and to extend it further will also be adequately taken care of.

HORTICULTURE

The horticulture sector is one of the focused sectors in the 11th Plan period. The basic objectives in this sector would be to provide modern technology for crop cultivation to the small and marginal farmers, ensure improved pre and post harvest management and arrange for processing and marketing of different products from the sector.

Farmers will be made aware of the improved practices for the cultivation of horticultural crops and encouraged to diversify from traditional crops to plantations, orchards, vineyards, flowers, fruits, medicinal and aromatic plants.

Joint sector projects for the production of hybrid seeds for different horticultural products will be promoted without interfering with the environment.

The number of pack houses, cold storages, cold chains will also be increased significantly.

Availability of good quality planting materials will be ensured through setting up of progeny orchards, nurseries, etc. Additional numbers of Agri-Export Zones for different products will also be set up and the proposed ones for cashew nuts and floriculture etc. will be followed up vigorously.

As already noted, post-harvest infrastructure will be developed either through private investments or PPP. NABARD schemes in this area will be given special attention. As much of these infrastructures could have multiple uses, the possibility of co-promotion of these infrastructures with animal husbandry, fishery, agri-marketing and agricultural departments will be explored. Similarly, vigorous extension services will be pursued in the horticulture sector to promote modern production techniques.

Every effort will be made to increase the flow of investments to the food processing industry. The state has already made significant headway in this sector and the achievements already made will be sustained through appropriate policy measures and promotional activities.

The availability of adequate and cheap credit will be a major initiative for marginal and small farmers to thrive. In recent years, the flow of credit to the agricultural sector has improved. In 2004-05, Rs. 1962.53 crores of credit was provided to the agriculture sector, which was 80.46 per cent of the target. In 2005-06, the flow of credit to the agriculture sector was Rs. 2970 crores, this was 83 per cent of the target. It will be ensured that the flow increases in the 11th Plan.

Restructuring and the strengthening of the cooperative sector will be expedited as the efficient functioning of the sector is crucial to the overall rural growth during the 11th Plan. This apart, the role of SHGs has become increasingly important in providing micro-credit in the rural areas. The State Government will take full advantage of the Central Government initiatives in this regard and ensure that the SHGs could access to the credit from the banking sector.

IRRIGATION

Major Irrigation

In the major irrigation sector, the Teesta Barrage Project (TBP) has the target for creating irrigation potential of 5.27 lakh hectares. This is the biggest on-going irrigation project in the country. Given that TBP project seeks to create irrigation potential in the six backward North Bengal districts, the project is of national importance and should be funded by the Central Government. Moreover, if even a part of the Subarnarekha Barrage Project (SBP) is taken up under the Bharat Nirman programme, it will be a big leap-forward. This apart, new avenues will be explored to harness irrigation potentials as a step towards maximizing output in this sector.

The necessity to carry out flood control measures has created a fund crunch and the state is finding it difficult to execute the maintenance and repair of existing major and medium irrigation of projects. Thus, apart from the Subarnarekha Barrage project, extension, renovation and modernization of a few components of completed major and medium irrigation require to be included in Bharat Nirman Programme. The funding pattern under the Bharat Nirman Programme should be 75 per cent (grant of Government of India) and 25 per cent state's share.

As the emphasis in the 11th Plan will be on the utilization of surface water on an increasing scale, special importance will be given to the completion of the 7 on-going medium irrigation schemes. A number of other medium irrigation projects will also be taken up. Instead of concentrating on large irrigation projects, which takes years to complete and are difficult to finance, it would be the attempt of the State Government to take up some medium irrigation projects. These will allow the creation of additional irrigation potential in a very short time.

Minor Irrigation

In the minor irrigation sector every effort will be made to prevent the over-exploitation of the ground water. In this context, the West Bengal Ground Water Resources (Management, Control and Regulation) Act, 2005 will be effectively implemented to control the misuse of ground water sources. Water harvesting tanks, percolation tanks, etc. will be effectively used in checking surface runoffs during monsoon and help in the conservation of surface water and in recharging the underlying aquifer.

The inclusion of minor irrigation projects proposed by the state and also the Repair, Renovation and Restoration of Water Bodies

Scheme under the Bharat Nirman Programme would give a fillip to the development of minor irrigation potential in the state.

In addition, the matter of sanctioning of the World Bank financed minor irrigation project as well as the Government of Japan financed similar project will be taken up with the Government of India. Attempt will be made to begin these projects in the early years of the 11th Plan. Project for Accelerated Development for Minor Irrigation (ADMI) for creating additional irrigation potentials is also sought to be implemented in the state with the assistance of the Government of India.

The envisaged Centrally Sponsored Project of Artificial Recharge to Ground Water and Rain Water Harvesting will not be confined to the districts of Bankura, Purulia and Paschim Midnapore but extended to Blocks where ground water assessment has shown that complete recuperation of ground water has not been achieved after the monsoon.

The process of handing over minor irrigation schemes set up by the public sector agencies in consultation with the Panchayats to the beneficiaries for operation and maintenance will be accelerated. Guidelines will be provided to these committees on the basis of an assessment of their functioning.

ANIMAL RESOURCES

As of now, the production of different animal husbandry products in the state is too inadequate to meet the minimum nutritional norms for these products. The usual policy of stock upgradation, providing health care and arranging for feed, have been trotted out over the successive plans. However, these measures have not resulted in a marked development of the sector.

The cost of concentrates and other annual feed in the state is on the higher side. It is necessary to formulate alternative fodder policy so that farmers have access to cheap feed which will allow them to take up cattle rearing on a profitable basis. This apart, the 11th Plan will attempt the development of adequate infrastructures for milk processing and milk collection. The best practices in other parts of the country will be effectively utilized.

In the poultry sector, high cost of feed also constrains the growth of layers since they have to be fed for a longer period than the broilers. This erodes the profitability of layer rearing. It has to be seen that cheap poultry feed is made available. In formulating policy on cheap cattle and poultry feed the assistance of experts and universities will be taken.

FISHERY

In the fishery sector the coverage by the FFDA of water bodies each year needs to be enhanced. There is a perceptible decline in the pace of extending fish farming to hitherto unutilized water bodies. Of the total 2.76 lakh hectares of impounded water area, about 70 to 79 per cent is presently under fish culture. In other water bodies the utilization is much lower except for sewage fed fisheries. Fuller utilization of these water bodies at a rapid rate will considerably improve the rate of growth in fish production. The 11th Plan's objective will be to address this area seriously.

Considerable development of the infrastructure for the fishery sector is necessary. With a developed infrastructure in place, the state could look for markets outside the state. Although the state has been exporting prawns, fish production dependence on other states for meeting domestic requirement of fish will have to be reduced through accelerated growth of fish production. The scope for food processing in the fishery sector will also be explored.

SUNDERBANS DEVELOPMENT

Sunderbans is a backward deltaic region. The major problems in this region are inadequate communication facilities and limited livelihood opportunities.

In Sunderbans, 45 per cent of the population belongs to the backward communities against the state average of 28.5 per cent. Only 12 per cent of the cultivable land is irrigated and the cropping intensity is only 120 against 180 for the state. Thus most of the area is mono-cropped.

Although 85 per cent of the population in the region depends on agriculture, only 30 per cent of the workforce is actually employed in agriculture. The unemployed workforce is 63 per cent of the population. It also ensures programme convergence of other plan implementing departments working in North Bengal. The Special Area Programme has been fairly successful in improving the regional balance.

During the Eleventh Five Year Plan the priorities of the Uttarbanga Unnayan Parishad would be as follows:

- Agriculture and Minor Irrigation,
- Irrigation and Flood Control,
- Soil Conservation,
- Industry—Small Scale and Agro-based Industries,
- Infrastructure Development—Roads, Bridges, Culverts, Drains etc.,
- System equipment—Power Supply,
- Education Sector—Construction of Schools and Colleges, and
- Health Infrastructure for the improvement of health services and health care facilities.

RURAL DEVELOPMENT

The successful implementation of the rural development programmes is integral to the involvement of the rural poor through the three tiers of the Panchayat system in formulating implementing and monitoring of schemes. The state has a functioning decentralized planning system for over two decades. The State Government is determined to further consolidate the achievements in this area and to create enabling situation for wider participation of the people in the whole process so that the benefits of the RD programmes enhance the capabilities of the people with the empowerment of the people, particularly the women and weaker sections as the central focus.

In the rural development sector a plethora of schemes like SGRY, SGSY, NREGP, IAY, PMGSY, PROFLAL, RSVY, etc. is being implemented with the involvement of the Panchayats. All these schemes are important and crucial for attaining the objectives of expanding livelihood opportunities and alleviating rural poverty. As the on going Strengthening of Rural Decentralization (SRD) project (in operation in 304 Blocks of six districts) has already revealed, there is, *inter alia*, considerable scope for strengthening the capacity of the Panchayats at all levels; its scope will be fully explored. Similarly, the district and state level administration relevant to decentralized planning will also be strengthened substantially. SHGs will also be involved in the whole process of rural development. Capacity building, empowerment, manpower development and strengthening of resource base will be vigorously pursued for sustainable development as well as to help the rural economy emerge stronger besides making the Panchayat System the symbol of people's collective choice and freedom.

Rural Water Supply

The state has set the target of covering all 'scarcity' (i.e. not covered or partially covered) habitations by March 2007 and quality affected habitations (i.e. arsenic, fluoride, saline affected ground water) by March 2012.

Efforts will be made to achieve the targets through intensified initiatives and inter-departmental coordination particularly the PHE, H&FW, School Education, P&RD Departments. The harvesting of rainwater and after proper filtration using it as drinking water specially in contaminated ground water will also be considered. In the arsenic affected areas, awareness of the people of the problems of arsenic or fluoride contamination will also be ensured. The involvement of the people through GP/ULB in arsenic mitigation schemes will be given special attention. R&D efforts will be intensified to develop a system for the disposal of arsenic affected sludge from arsenic removal systems.

Sanitation

It is expected that around 75 per cent or a little more of the rural households will have sanitary toilets by the end of the 10th Plan. During the 11th Plan, the remaining 25 per cent or a little less of the households without sanitary latrines will be covered expectedly within the first two years. It is expected that all schools will be provided with sanitary latrines by the end of the 10th Plan. However, it is apprehended that separate toilets for boys and girls in each and every school might not be possible within the 10th Plan period. The 11th Plan, therefore, envisages the construction of separate sanitary latrines for boys and girls in the schools, qualitative improvement of existing toilets will also be carried out. New schools being set up will also be provided with toilets and drinking water sources.

Moreover, an important aspect of the strategy in this sector is to provide clean and convenient 'lifeline' energy for the well being of the poor even when they cannot fully pay for it. It will endeavour to promote the balanced development of the energy sector based on optimum utilization of resources such as coal, natural gas, hydro, renewable sources of energy and nucleus substances or materials.

Rural Electrification

West Bengal's performance on the electrification of villages has not reached the expected level. Rural electrification has been included in the Bharat Nirman Programme of the Central Government. The national target for rural electrification is to electrify all villages by the end of 2007-08 and provide universal access to all households by March, 2010. Under the Rajiv Gandhi Grameen Vidyutikaran Yojana (RGGVY) electrification of 5000 unelectrified villages in the state has been taken up as a crash programme. However, achieving universalization of access in the rural areas by 2010 will be quite difficult. But, every effort will be made to achieve the deadline. The progress of this programme is being closely monitored. The State Government will fully explore the potential of non-conventional energy sources for the areas without access to conventional power service level comparable to those covered under the conventional power system.

Bio-Fuel Policy

The depletion of oil reserves, national security considerations on dependence on imports and its increasing cost and the urge for diminished non-toxic fallouts call for alternative sources of energy to reduce our dependence on fossil fuels. Bio-fuel is gaining wide acceptance as an environment-friendly and cost-effective alternative energy resource. It is a renewable liquid fuel and self-sustaining besides being suitable under our soil conditions and gifting valuable organic manure as a by-product. Bio-diesel produced from *jatropha* etc. mixed with petro-diesel extends the engine life. Additionally, this wasteland-friendly lower gestation period agricultural crop improves soil character and meets the social objective of employment creation. The global market for bio-diesel is poised for explosive growth and it is possible that as much as 20 per cent of all on-road diesel could be met from this source.

Having regard to the potential of bio-fuel the state would design its separate bio-fuel policy.

During the Eleventh Five Year Plan, focused efforts would be made to make use of all sources of bio-fuels including *jatropha* for sharing a considerable burden of our energy load and for value addition to the growth of the rural economy. Fox extending *jatropha* cultivation the state would tie-up National Rural Employment Guarantee Schemes initiatives along with other State Plan initiatives.

The State Government has already initiated a programme to set up 10000 'family size' biogas plants every year. The West Bengal Renewable Energy Development Agency, formed in 1993, has a mandate to promote renewable energy technologies and ensure their commercialization through innovative projects.

At present, WBREDA has two major bio-fuel programmes in the state, one is the setting up of cattle dung based biogas plants and the other is rice husk based gasifier plants. Apart from electricity generation, research is also being carried out to use bio-fuel agricultural waste in the transport sector as clean fuel.

MEDICINAL AND AROMATIC PLANTS

There is a demand for the supply of medicinal and aromatic plants for use by various pharmaceutical companies. Problems lie in the market being unregulated with the big buyers bothering more about cost rather than being quality conscious. Efforts have been made by the West Bengal State Medicinal Plant Board for the large companies to register the source of materials. Focus should also be on growing the plants without chemicals to avoid residues in the finished products. Major plants of interest include Sarpagandha, Aswagandha, Thankuni, Kalmegh, Chiraita, Zinger, Turmeric, Ghritakumari, Tulsi, Citronella, Neem, Brahmi, Pudina, Amloki, Nayantara, Anantamul, etc. along with the requirement of standard quality materials and sustainable cultivation procedures. There is also the need for correct identification of the plant materials by trained experts. The people of rural areas can be assisted through training and motivating in the conservation, cultivation, harvesting and processing of medicinal and aromatic plants. Marketing of products has to be facilitated through buy-back arrangements with the end users.

CHASH-O-BASABASER BHUMIDAN PROKALPA

The State Government will make the most of the programmes during the 11th Plan by adopting strategies suited to the ground realities. Chash-O-Basabaser Bhumidan Prokalpa, i.e. CBBP (homestead and kitchen garden) will also be introduced in the state plan during the 11th Plan. The scheme seeks to assist the houseless and homesteadless poor families, specially those belonging to the SC/ST communities. Rs. 2000 will be spent on each family. Another scheme for the construction of houses for artisans having no land of their own will also be taken up. It is targeted to provide 20000 artisan families with homestead land each year. This programme will be dovetailed with IAY. The problem of no homestead land for eligible households under IAY could be overcome by the provision of land under CBBP.

Improving the primary health sector is a priority area. Fund for this has been obtained by pooling financial resources from the state plan, National Rural Health Mission (NRHM), KFW assisted Basic Health Project, EC assisted Sector Improvement Project and DFID financed Health System Development Initiative. Construction of large number of sub-centres and their recognization is in progress. A second ANM is being engaged in each sub-centre as per the guidelines under NRHM. Work on converting 342 Primary Health Centres into 10 bedded hospitals with 24 hours service facilities is going on. The upgradation of the Block Primary Health Centres to 30-40 bedded facilities has also commenced. Commensurate expansion of higher level of health facilities will also be taken up. It is also the objective of the State Government to create state-of-the-art health facilities to cater to the needs of the people. The initiatives taken during the 10th Plan will be completed during the 11th Plan. Apart from developing various sectors of the Health Systems, modern system of Health Management inclusive of IT based Health Manager Information System in all secondary and tertiary level hospitals will be fully utilized. Private investment in the health sector will be encouraged and modern facilities will be extended to every nook and corner. The 11th Plan's focus is 'health for all people'.

EDUCATION

Literacy in the state has substantially increased. In rural West Bengal literacy has increased to 67.4 per cent of the 7 + rural population in the first half of 2004 from 63.4 per cent in 2001 (census). Urban literacy has increased to 86.4 per cent in 2004 from 81.25 per cent in 2001. And overall literacy has increased to 69.22 per cent in 2004, as per SSA Report from 68.64 per cent in 2001.

As on 1 April 2006 as per the SSA Report, the net enrolment ratio was 98.03 per cent at the primary level and 78.74 per cent at the upper primary level, given this position the state hopes to achieve the objective of the universalization of elementary education well before 2010.

In the 11th Plan the following basic objectives have been set for the school education:

1. Try to ensure universalization of secondary education,
2. All out efforts for the elimination of existing social and gender gaps in school education,
3. Ensure better quality of education at all levels, and
4. Converge all resources from different sources to finance the development of school education.

At the primary level the objectives for the 11th Plan are:

1. To bring all the schools, gram sansad and wards under the coverage of SSAs.
2. To create resource centres at all levels from the state to the gram sansad level.
3. To strengthen the process for the involvement of the parents and the community in primary education so as to improve the quality of education.
4. Involve PRIs in the management and planning for primary schools.

5. To fill up vacancies of teachers and create posts for teachers for ensuring 40 : 1 pupil-teacher ratio.
6. To pay special attention to the disadvantaged groups like SC/ST, linguistic and religious minorities, educationally backward areas/communities and physically handicapped children in order to bridge the social gap in education.
7. To effect convergence between the ICDS and primary education so as to allow automatic transition from pre-primary to class I.
8. To increase the enrolment and retention of the girl students.
9. SSA support to SSK and opening of similar short-term study centres in order to bridge the gaps in access to primary schools.

In addition, at the upper primary level the following aspects will be given due emphasis:

1. Extend support of the SSA upto class VIII to all junior high and H.S. schools including Madarasas.
2. To improve the functioning of the District Institute for Education and Training (DIETs) so that the scope for the training of teachers is expanded and qualitatively improved.
3. Improve the infrastructure facilities not only at the upper primary level but also at the secondary and higher secondary level.
4. To extend the mid-day meal scheme upto the upper primary level in the first instance and then to the secondary level after due evaluation and monitoring.
5. Upgrade upper primary schools and Madarasas so as to increase the capacity of the higher level of school education.

GENDER PLAN

In tune with faster and more inclusive growth the state would have distinct and focused Gender Plan to address the gender related issues, programme outreach and level of social and woman-empowerment. All cross-sectoral issues under the Gender Plan would be coordinated and the convergence of programme initiatives ensured in partnership with civil society both at the state level and also at the decentralized levels. To this end there would also be a decentralized Gender Plan under the District Plan and also in all tiers of the Panchayat and the Municipality/Corporation Plan. The following items are intended to be addressed under the Gender Plan:

- Gender Literacy drive to bridge Gender Gap in education.
- A special programme like the National Programme of Education for Girls at Elementary Level (NPEGEL) has been running to intensify the need-based delivery mechanism for promoting the girls education and reducing the gender gap.
- A new programme, Kasturba Gandhi Balika Vidyalaya, has been launched in the educationally backward blocks providing residential facilities for the girl students.
- Improving infrastructural facilities like separate toilets, boundary walls, etc. for the co-educational/girls schools.
- Special programme for remedial teaching, book grant, merit scholarship, etc.
- Enlarging need-based hostel facility.
- Institutionalizing vocational education at the school level and business orientation as required.
- Intensifying special focus on skill development programmes having marketable linkage.
- Dissemination of livelihood related options including wage employment, self-employment, pension and others available for the women having regard to education, skill, age, special category, etc.
- Arranging sale-outlets/market complex for the products of the women's groups.
- Organizing gender friendly institutional delivery units in partnership with the Government and Non-Government service providers. Promotion of village based trained '*dais*' in remote areas.
- Mobilization of social support on dangers of too early pregnancies and child marriage.
- Ensuring complete stoppage of female foeticide by strict implementation of the preconception and PNDT Act.

- Updated ECCR based prenatal and antenatal care including other health support care for the mother and the children.
- Special focus on adolescent care and nutrition.
- Organizing institutional care of Short Stay Homes, Destitute Homes, Day Care Homes, Old Age Homes, crèches, etc.
- Decentralized counselling network for protection issues related to women including domestic violence, trafficking, harassment at workplaces, dowry and other related issues, etc.
- Forming local bodies specific unit for tackling the migration of women.
- Awareness of dangers of HIV and AIDS related issues.
- Gender disaggregated data for all issues relating to women.

INTEGRATED CHILD DEVELOPMENT SERVICES

One of the most important programmes being implemented in the state for women and children is the Integrated Child Development Services (ICDS). At present there are 55000 *Anganwadi* Centres and 17100 additional centres will be operationalized in 2006-07.

There is a move to sanction 17500 additional *Anganwadi* Centres for ITDP *mouzas*, Sunderbans and for Darjeeling. At present 37.54 lakh children in the age group 6 months to 6 years and 4.55 lakh pregnant and lactating mothers benefit from the ICDS. The most important programme under the ICDS is the Supplementary Nutrition Programme (SNP) for children (6 months to 6 years) and pregnant and lactating mothers. The ICDS programme also provides pre-primary schooling for children below 6 years.

At present 60 per cent of under 6 children and 54 per cent of eligible mothers attend *Anganwadi* Centres and are given cooked meals fortified with vitamins. The coverage will be universalized. It is, therefore, proposed for an addition of 10000 *Anganwadi* Centres more during the 11th Plan. Special arrangements like opening of crèches, supply of take-home ready-to-eat nutritious food will have to be made for the children of poor working women. The feeding of lactating mothers at *Anganwadi* Centres will be extended to one year from 6 months at present in order to motivate mothers to attend *Anganwadi* Centres. Thus, both mothers and children would get fortified food for one year. This will reduce absenteeism of the children in age group 6 months to 1 year in the *Anganwadi* Centres. As a result, there will be more time for *Anganwadi* workers to teach the mothers the benefit of breast-feeding and the importance of nutritious food. The State Government will also make special efforts to improve the infrastructure for the ICDS programme in the 11th Plan. Special emphasis will be given on the welfare of children (below 14 years) who have to work for their livelihood.

The operation of Integrated Street/Working Children programme at present is confined to Kolkata and Howrah. This will be extended to other districts. Moreover, the following measures will be taken:

(i) Infrastructure improvement of *Anganwadi* Centres and clubbing them with health sub-centres wherever it is possible.

(ii) Converting *Anganwadi* Centres from mere feeding centres to centres for comprehensive care of children.

(iii) Improving sanitation and hygiene at home schools by increasing the availability of safe water and sanitary toilets. Increasing awareness of poor families for the need for more hygienic environment.

(iv) Strengthening pre-school education in *Anganwadi* Centres.

The fact of regional disparities and imbalances has been one of the major areas of concern in West Bengal. Successful implementation of the Rashtriya Sam Vikas Yojana (RSVY) during the 10th Plan period in the districts of Purulia, Jalpaiguri, Paschim Medinipur, Uttar Dinajpur, Dakshin Dinajpur, Bankura, Birbhum and South 24-Parganas has yielded positive results in this direction. It is hoped that with RSVY being subsumed into the Backward Regions Grant Fund (BRGF), having more districts within its ambit, the state will be able to address the problems in the pockets of backwardness, to a large extent, by the end of the plan period.

Gender inequality is another sector in which the State Government has planned to focus attention. To this end, the State Government has brought out a report on Gender Budgeting in

November 2006. Based on the inputs the state plans to garner its resources towards the removal of this factor of social acrimony.

Generation of employment in West Bengal is being planned in a two-pronged reduction of unemployment and removal of under-employment. With the formation of Self Help Groups (SHGs) and the ushering in of industrialization, the State Government plans to achieve the target of sustainable employment during the Eleventh Five Year Plan. Diversification in the micro and small scale sector enterprises, capacity building and skill development of artisans and craftsmen can improve this process.

GRAM SANSAD PLANS IN WEST BENGAL

West Bengal is a pioneer in decentralized planning in the country. The kernel of the Gram Sansad Plan is CCA (Convergent Community Action).

CCA is such a process of development, where people and coordinators of development play the role of partners. Under this system, the coordinators have to believe that they cannot uplift the people. They could work as a helper or a partner in the process of development. But in reality, the picture is different. Most of the coordinators do not have the desire to play the role of a helper. One associated with development once said that as a coordinator they are the only knowledgeable persons, and the people do not know anything. Even people believe that only we know, but they themselves do not know anything. But both the parties do not realize that the coordinators also do not know.

But the truth lies elsewhere. Both the coordinators and the people have the knowledge and experience. Even those who are not formally educated have also got knowledge and experience. They are creative and have traditional skills, which may not be appreciated by the coordinators of development. On the other hand the coordinators have knowledge due to education and ability and due to opportunity and experience. If the knowledge, experience and skills of both the partners are exchanged and used in the process of development then it can gain momentum and cause lasting benefits. Both the partners could increase their level of knowledge, experience and skills to usher in an all round development.

If both the partners join hands, the result will definitely be good but otherwise the work might be affected. Let us consider that a Panchayat Samiti has decided to construct a sluice gate on the feeder canal of a big dam. Only local people could tell about the volume of water that had gone down the stream over the last few years. No engineer from outside can ascertain it correctly without the assistance of the local people. Under the circumstances the said engineer should not plan the structure of the gate without consulting the local people. On the other hand the villagers cannot take any technical decision about the size and strength of the sluice gate, which could withstand the pressure of flood water. So, if the villagers decide to construct such a sluice gate they should consult a technocrat who has sufficient knowledge in this regard.

This is the basic concept of CCA. The CCA considers primarily the development of those people who are most backward, though it brings benefits to all sections of people, directly or indirectly. The other important feature is that CCA does not speak about the participation of people in the development work, being undertaken by the government agencies or Panchayats. On the contrary, CCA speaks about the participation of the government agencies or Panchayats in the people's own process of development.

Convergent Community Planning (CCP)

It is needless to say that the basis of CCA is also the foundation of CCP. It is imperative to establish CCP for successful implementation of CCA. The sole purpose of CCP is that the stake holders themselves would formulate their plans and the coordinators would work as assistants in implementing those plans. CCP does not consider the 'association or participation' of the people. On the contrary, the coordinators would share their responsibility and power with the people and act as their partners. In the process of CCP, people themselves conceive, carry and coordinate the entire activities.

But the coordinators should realize the importance of being a partner and assistant in the entire process. If they could act accordingly, one should appreciate it as their capacity building. The first step towards training in formulating plans, is to emphasize on capacity building.

Traditional Planning and Development *vs.* CCP

Traditional Development and Planning	*CCD and Planning Process*
Least involvement of the common people	Beneficiaries are active and in the midst of everything
Ideas and decisions are imposed from top	Importance is given to the ideas and proposals which are considered at the grassroots level
Attempts are made at the top to improve the lot of the common people, but the fruits of development do not reach the desired level	Importance is given to the development of the poor and backward people, women and children. As a result, the fruits of development are within their reach
Dependence on officials	Dependence on local bodies
Short-lived development	Works for long term development
A few are responsible and answerable	All are responsible
Answerable and responsible only to the bosses	Primarily answerable to the people
A stereotyped formula for easy solution for every region—no scope for divergent views	Local needs and professions are considered in formulating local plans which is unique in nature
Officials of development and planning are at drivers' seat	People are partners in development and the officials act as assistants to the process of development
Emphasis is given on 'associating' people	Sharing of responsibility with the local people and organizations and in the process people are 'associated'
Success is measured in terms of spending financial allocations and meet the target set from the top	Success is measured in terms of formulating and implementing plans drawn in keeping with the local needs and available resources

The positive experience gathered from the initiatives taken for spreading the decentralized planning and CCA throughout the state are as follows:

- The experience of villagers in Midnapur district while drawing village plans in 1980.
- Experience from the watershed management undertaken at the end of 1990s.
- Experience gathered from the CCA.

- Experience from implementing decentralized planning in Midnapur, Jalpaiguri and Bardhaman districts.
- Recent experience of GP planning on the basis of Gram Sansad in six villages of five districts (Marnai and Dhankail in North Dinajpur, Sukdebpur in South Dinajpur, Hura in Purulia, Raghunathpur-1 in East Midnapur and Siakahala in Hooghly district).

Role of the Gram Sansad

(a) In view of the local planning, *Gram Panchayat* (GP) is quite a big area. At the same time a locality or a cluster of houses becomes too small a unit for preparing a plan for all-round development of a village. 'Social village', where people stay or '*Moujas*' may not be equal in size with the entire electoral constituency of a GP. As a result GS is the right basic unit as it is synonymous with the electoral constituency of the GP and has transparency and accountability. Only at this level all adult villagers can participate directly and take the responsibility of formulating a plan.

(b) Outsiders—trained employees and experts—usually conduct survey in a stereotyped format for the purpose of planning. These traditional surveys are costly and time consuming. Moreover, outsiders cannot understand properly the real problems, resources and potentials of a village. On the contrary, the villagers themselves could well identify their problems, resources and potentials, then analyse and evaluate them and fix the priorities. This does not take much time and costs little and often no cost is involved. The most important factor of this survey is that the villagers become aware of development and planning and could assume able leadership in the entire process. This exercise is possible only at the GS level.

(c) GS is such a tier of planning, where the poor and most backward people could participate. They can, jointly with their neighbours, raise their unheard and weak voices which is not possible in the GP or Panchayat Samiti. If plans are made to uplift the poor and most backward people, the exercise is to start at the GS level. But it does not mean that the village development committee will centrally discuss all the issues concerning planning and development for all the areas under the said GS. A GS might consist of a number of localities or villages and a part of a big village. Though at the grassroots, GS would be the unit of planning, discussions will be held in villages, localities and bustees under the same GS.

(d) In the rural areas, a number of local groups are involved in different development and social work. Survey revealed that a number of organizations function in a GS area: (1) the village education committee to undertake Sarba Siksha Abhiyan, (2) literacy committee for literacy campaign and continuous education, (3) committee for public health and total healthcare, (4) committee to run *Anganwadi*, (5) committee to run child education centre, (6) committee to run schools for child labour, (7) committee for minor-irrigation, (8) cooperative agricultural societies, (9) forest protection committee, (10) committee to manage local *hats* and markets, (11) transformer maintenance committee, (12) committee for the supply of piped water, (13) a number of self help groups, (14) sports and cultural organizations, (15) NGO and other voluntary organizations, (16) a number of political and social workers, peasants, youths and women's organizations. All these institutions are to be involved in formulating plans and this is possible only at the GS level.

Principal Areas of GS Planning

GP planning on the basis of GS plans has gained momentum in a number of districts. This process of planning is also based on the principles of involving village people. In some places (as in West Midnapur) 'area-wise planning' is quite popular. But it has certain risks involved. There might be a tendency to confine the total rural development plan within the framework of 'area-wise planning'. And as a result, the scope of spreading the ideas beyond the 'area-wise planning' may be restricted.

The common people believe that development means the development of infrastructure. It is learnt from experience that given the options to take independent decisions, the common people and even members of the panchayats would like to utilize government allocations for the development of infrastructure. However, 'area-wise planning' should not mean a separate plan of the development of a particular sector. On the contrary, the plan of a particular area would be complementary to the others. Experience shows that there is nothing wrong in laying emphasis on major areas at the GS level. The main areas of development under the GS may be (a) education, (b) public health, (c) women and child development, (d) agriculture and allied issues, (e) industry, (f) infrastructure and (g) other various areas.

Participatory Learning and Action or PLA Methods

There are three benefits of this method. First, by the application of PLA methods, one can collect different types of information quite easily and in the shortest possible time. Secondly, if information is collected by this method, it is possible to maintain quality and certainty of the information. Thirdly, by this method, the participation of people is increased. PLA is the part and parcel of the CCA. It is such a process, by means of which, both local people and convenors of planning and development can increase their knowledge, expertise and experience through discussions and subsequently analyse them and then quite easily, prepare plans, implement, supervise and evaluate them.

This method could be applied easily and in the process both villagers and surveyors can increase their knowledge and awareness about the variety of life and livelihood, problems and resources. PLA methods are to be applied for the GS Planning.

Conditions for the 'pro-poor', decentralized and participatory planning at GS:

If a GS plan can fulfil certain conditions then only it can be termed 'pro-poor' and participatory.

- Mass initiative is taken to organize campaign in localities for increasing awareness among the people and ensuring their participation and self help groups are constituted as preliminary work.
- With the assistance of the members of the VDS (Village Development Society) meetings are organized in different localities and by applying PLA methods all informations are collected and the plans are made on the basis of definite facts.

- Most of the villagers have actively participated in the planning exercise and promised to make contribution of time, labour, goods and cash at the time of implementation.
- Most of the members of the VDS have actively and regularly participated in the workshops and meetings regarding the plan.
- The members of the VDS or any other institution or agency have not tried to lord over the villagers and imposed any decision on them. On the contrary, decisions were taken on the basis of a consensus among the villagers after exchange of ideas and opinions.
- Opinions of the people, who are not supporters of the ruling parties, were considered with due importance at the time of taking decisions and it was reflected in the plan.
- Poor and most backward people like SC/ST, OBC and minorities, handicapped women in general and especially the women of the backward families have actively taken part in the local meetings and voiced their problems, necessities and priorities and their needs are accorded due place in the GS plan.
- With a view to ushering in education, health and other social developments of the poor and most backward people and creating employment opportunities for them, most of the works are selected and major part of allocations are earmarked.
- Different aspects of this plan are amply discussed at the meetings of the GS and while formulating the plan, transparency, honesty and unbiased attitude are shown.
- The Gram Panchayat as an institution has given all assistance at different stages of planning at the GS level and subsequently GS plan is incorporated in the GP plan.
- The plan has shown definite commitment towards establishing the ownership of the villagers in case of implementation, supervision and evaluation of the GS plan.

3

Orissa

S. TRIPATHY and JAI SINGH SHEKHAWAT

Orissa is divided into ten agro-climatic zones with varied characteristics. Its land can be classified into three categories: low (25.6%), medium (33.6%) and up-lands (40.8%) with various types of soil like red, yellow, red-loamy, alluvial, coastal alluvial, laterite, black soil, etc. with low and medium texture. The characteristics of different agro-climatic zones in Orissa are presented in Table 3.1.

Table 3.1: Agro-climatic Zones of Orissa

Sl. No.	*Agro-climatic Zone*	*Alimate*	*Mean Annual Rainfall (in mm)*	*Soil Group*
1.	North western plateau	Hot and moist	1648	Red and yellow
2.	North central plateau	Hot and moist	1535	Red loamy
3.	North eastern coastal plateau	Hot and moist sub-humid	1568	Alluvial
4.	East and south eastern plateau	Hot and moist	1449	Coastal alluvial saline (near the coast line)
5.	North eastern *ghat*	Hot and moist sub-humid	1597	Laterite and brown forest
6.	Eastern *ghat* high land	Warm and humid	1522	Red, brown
7.	South eastern *ghat*	Warm and humid	1522	Red, mixed red and yellow
8.	Western undulating	Warm and humid	1527	Black, mixed red and black
9.	West central table-land	Hot and moist	1527	Red, heavy textured colours
10.	Mid-central table-land	Hot and dry sub-humid	1421	Red loamy, laterite, mixed red and black

The state is rich in both renewable and non-renewable resources. The long coast line (480 km), the largest brackish water lagoon, i.e. Chilika Lagoon and a large number of water bodies in interior Orissa provide substantial potential for marine and brackish water fish production.

As per land utilization statistics—2004-05, 36.86 per cent of land is under cultivation and 37.33 per cent under forest cover, while about 6.41 per cent of land has been put to non-agricultural uses. The details of the land-use pattern during 2004-05 are summarized in Table 3.2.

Table 3.2: Land Utilization Pattern of Orissa—2004-05

Sl. No.	Land Use Pattern	Area in '000 hectare	Percentage to Total Area
1.	Forest Area	5.813	37.33
2.	Miscellaneous Trees and Grooves	482	3.10
3.	Permanent Pasture	443	2.84
4.	Culturable Waste	392	2.52
5.	Land put to non-agricultural use	999	6.41
6.	Barren and unculturable land	843	5.41
7.	Current Fallow	426	2.74
8.	Other Fallow	434	2.79
9.	Net Area Sown	5.739	36.86
	Total Geographical Area	15571	100

DEMOGRAPHY

The population of the state, according to the 2001 census, is 368.05 lakh which is about 3.58 per cent of the population of the country. The decennial growth rate of population of 16.25 per cent in the state during the decade 1991-2001 was much lower than the growth rate of 20.06 per cent during the previous decade (1981-1991). The sex ratio of 971 females per 1000 males in 1991 marginally increased to 972 in 2001 which is much higher than the corresponding all India figures of 927 and 933 respectively. The total literacy rate in the state which was 49.09 per cent during 1991 has increased to 63.08 per cent in 2001 census. The female literacy rate has also increased remarkably from 34.68 to 50.51 per cent during the same period.

The census data reveal that, while the percentage of total workers to total population in the state has increased from 37.53 per cent in

1991 to 38.79 per cent in 2001, the percentage of main workers to total workers has declined from 87.33 to 67.17 per cent. This indicates that the extent of under-employment in the state has considerably increased. The proportion of male workers to male population and female workers to female population in the state, as per the 2001 census stood at 52.5 per cent and 24.7 per cent respectively while corresponding proportions at the all India level were 51.7 per cent and 25.6 per cent respectively.

IRRIGATION

Although the state has excellent irrigation potential with around 11.00 per cent of the country's total surface water resources, the same has not been harnessed fully. The net irrigation potential created by the end of 2005-06 from all sources was 27.51 lakh hectares, which is 46.63 per cent of the estimated irrigable area of the state. Out of this, 45.4 per cent was covered through major and medium irrigation, 18.8 per cent through minor (flow) irrigation, 4.3 per cent by minor (lift) irrigation and balance 21.5 per cent through other sources. The total cultivated area covered under irrigation till the end of 2004-05 was 47.33 per cent.

Participatory Irrigation Management in the form of Pani Panchayats has been adopted as a policy for the development of the water resource sector. 13284 Pani Panchayats have been formed till the end of the year 2006 covering an area of 10.51 lakh hectares of which, 8.06 lakh hectares has been handed over to 11498 Pani Panchayats.

AGRICULTURAL PRODUCTION

Agriculture sector continues to be the backbone of state's economy contributing about a quarter of the total NSDP. While the contribution of agriculture sector to NSDP has come down to about 26 per cent now from a level of 67 per cent in 1951 there has not been much change in the workforce engaged in the sector. Even now around 64 per cent of the total workforce is dependent on agriculture which indicates that labour productivity is low in the sector.

The production of food grain in the state has increased from 51.04 lakh tonnes in 1970-71 to 73.59 lakh tonnes in 2005-06, but the increase in the yield rate of food grain from 847 kg/ha in 1970-71 to 1.154 kg/ha in 2004-05 is not very significant as compared to the national average yield rate of 1562 kg/ha in 2002-03.

Over dependence on paddy cultivation in rainfed condition is a limiting factor to agricultural growth because of the state's proneness to natural calamities and drought conditions. In terms of area, the share of paddy out of the net area sown, has reduced from 64.36 per cent in 1950-51 to 57.18 per cent in 2002-03, which is still quite high. Another major constraint to the adoption of modern agricultural practices in the state are the low level of capital formation and the small size of the operational holdings. The Orissa Agricultural Policy, 1996 of the State Government has addressed these issues and the overall agricultural production in the state has improved during the Tenth Plan.

REGIONAL AND SOCIAL DISPARITIES

Orissa is afflicted by acute regional, social and gender disparities which are the outcome of long-term neglect of depressed regions and 'entitlement failures' for marginalized sections. It is, therefore, desirable that institutional framework that protects 'entitlements' of the most disadvantaged sections of society should be strengthened. Many development programmes (e.g. education, health, food security and livelihood schemes) that have been implemented in the past have not worked well for the poor and in the depressed regions. It is, therefore, necessary that region and issue-based developmental schemes for depressed areas and disadvantaged sections need be developed on the basis of careful research and understanding of local level problems. One reason why various developmental programmes have not worked in the depressed regions is the failure of governance in these areas. Wide variations have been observed in human development and infrastructure development across the districts.

The State Government has recently taken several steps to address regional, social and gender disparities. Eight key initiatives have been taken to address the problem of underdevelopment and regional disparities include the Long-Term Action Plan (LTAP)/Revised Long-Term Action Plan (RLTAP) for KBK districts. The second initiative is the inclusion of 19 additional districts: Bolangir, Boudh Gaya,

Deogarh, Dhenkanal, Gajpati, Ganjam, Jharsuguda, Kalahandi, Kandhmal, Keonjhar, Koraput, Kalkangiri, Mayurbhanj, Nawarangpur, Nuapara, Rayagada, Sambalpur, Sonepur and Sundergarh under the 'Backward Regions Grant Fund (BRGF)'. Third, the State Government have also launched the Gopabandhu Gramin Yojana in 11 additional districts including Bargarh and coastal districts. Fourth, the Biju KBK Plan has been launched in the KBK districts to supplement development efforts under RLTAP. Fifth, Western Orissa Development Council (WODC) has been constituted for the backward districts of the western part of Orissa to quicken the pace of development in these districts. The sixth initiative is to bridge the critical infrastructure gaps in identified sectors in the TSP areas out of the grant-in-aid received under Article 275(1) of the Constitution. The seventh initiative is the implementation of development programmes in TSP areas funded out of Special Central Assistance. The eighth initiative is the establishment of the Regional Imbalance Enquiry Commission, headed by Justice S. K. Mohanty (Retd.), with a view to (i) conducting free and fair investigation into the existing regional imbalances in the development process of the state and its trend in terms of different socio-economic parameters like agriculture, infrastructure development, poverty, health care, literacy, population, employment, etc. and (ii) suggesting suitable measures to address the existing regional disparities as well as to halt this trend. Those not having this access, have been creating social tensions. Focused attention is, therefore, needed to address these problems and narrow gaps during the Eleventh Plan.

A VISION FOR THE FUTURE

The Approach Paper to the Eleventh Plan, approved by the NDC, aims at fostering faster and broad based inclusive growth in the economy during the Plan period. Keeping in view imperatives outlined in the Approach Paper for the Eleventh Plan and taking into account the gains and positive trends of the Tenth Plan and the challenges ahead, the following broad objectives have been drawn up for the Eleventh Plan for the state:

(i) A sustainable high growth rate of 9 per cent per annum is aimed.

(ii) Agricultural production will be doubled from its present level to realize a growth rate of about 5 per cent.

(iii) Significant improvement will be made in people's access to basic facilities like health care, education, clean drinking water and sanitation.

(iv) Special attention will be given to the welfare of the marginalized sections of the society, particularly the ST, SC and minority communities, adolescent girls, the elderly and the physically challenged persons, children below three years of age.

(v) Suitable policy measures to be taken to create a conducive environment that fosters the growth of entrepreneurship and encourages private sector investment.

(vi) Public sector investment will be stepped up particularly in the Agriculture, Infrastructure and Human Development sectors. Resources required will be mobilized, by the State Government, PSUs, PRIs/ULBs through the prudent management of finances and exploring new avenues for resource mobilization.

(vii) Focus will be on outcomes rather than on expenditure. Monitoring and evaluation of the Plan Programme will be substantially improved and made more effective to ensure that outlays and outputs are converted into outcomes.

(viii) The state's efforts will continue to maintain the pace of the industrialization process coupled with measures to achieve environmental sustainability and reducing human suffering due to displacement.

(ix) Efforts will also continue to bring significant improvements in all components of human development not only to reach the desirable standard but also to match the standard already achieved in the advanced states.

(x) Large-scale employment will be generated to absorb the backlog of the unemployed as well as new entrants to labour force. Because of the limited scope in the generation of regular organized sector employment, emphasis will be on the creation of self-employment avenues. The state's efforts to improve training facilities for improving the desired skills of the unemployed persons and ensure the availability of the right kind of manpower to meet the emerging requirements of the industries, service sector and agricultural sector.

(xi) Efforts will be made to bring about significant improvement in all components of the economic infrastructure, particularly the road connectivity. Apart from providing all weather connectivity to villages, efforts will be made to significantly improve the quality of existing road network to effectively support the upcoming industries. The state aims to connect all villages with 1000+ population in general and villages with 500+ population in tribal, hilly and interior pockets. District level connectivity Master Plans shall be developed and implemented.

(xii) For achieving high growth rate in agriculture, efforts will be made to step up irrigation potential substantially, ensuring maximum possible utilization of created irrigation potential. The state aims to ensure that each block has at least 35 per cent of the sown area to be irrigated during the 11th Plan.

(xiii) The sustained efforts of the state in the area of governance reforms will continue to improve the public service making public machinery more efficient, transparent and accountable. In this context, emphasis will be given on the adoption of e-governance.

(xiv) The fiscal reforms process will be continued to consolidate the gains and improve the resource base of the State Government for greater investment in the development programmes.

(xv) The sustained efforts of the State Government towards effective devolution of powers and responsibilities to the Panchayati Raj Institutions and Urban Local Bodies and decentralization of planning process will be further strengthened.

MONITORABLE TARGETS

In conformity with the continuing emphasis on physical outcomes rather than on financial outlays in the context of the implementation of the Plan programme, the concept of monitorable targets in Social Service Sector was introduced during the 10th Plan. Monitorable targets ensure that the key objectives of the plan may be quantified and specific targets may be fixed for their realization during the plan period. This helps better monitoring of the implementation and evaluation of the development programmes. Key monitorable targets for the 11th Plan, as approved by the National Development Council, for the following sectors: (i) Income and Poverty, (ii) Education, (iii) Health, (iv) Women and Child Welfare, (v) Infrastructure, and (vi) Environment have been adopted for both India and the states. The Planning Commission has already communicated the state specific monitorable targets in respect of 9 items for Orissa as indicated in the following table. The state will also strive to realize the targets agreed to at the national level in respect of the rest of the relevant items.

Table 3.3: Monitorable Targets for Orissa

Sl. No.	Monitorable Item	Units	Target for 11th Plan	
			For India	For Orissa
1.	Infant mortality rate	Per 1000 live births	28	37
2.	Maternity mortality Ratio	Per 1000 live births	1	1.19
3.	Total fertility rate	No. of children per couple	2.1	2.1
4.	Malnutrition of children (0-3 years)	Percentage of wt. for age below 2 SD	23.5	27.2
5.	Anemia among women 15-59 years	In per cent	28.3	31.5
6.	Sex ratio (0-6 years)	No. of female per 1000 male	977	961
7.	Drop-out rate in elementary education	In per cent	20	31.99
8.	Literacy rate	In per cent	85.00	83.96
9.	Gender gap in literacy	In percentage points	10.00	15.10

DEVELOPMENT STRATEGY FOR CERTAIN SECTORS

Agriculture

The plan envisages doubling agricultural production and aims to achieve a growth rate of about 5 per cent. This calls for improving agricultural productivity through the adoption of modern practices and at the same time insulating agricultural production from the uncertainty of the monsoon and natural calamities. Transforming the traditional agricultural practices, particularly in respect of crop diversification and adoption of modern techniques, requires making available all the appropriate inputs, changing of the farmers' mindset and bridging the knowledge gap. The extension machinery of the state will be geared up to meet these requirements. For reducing dependence on monsoon, irrigation facilities have to be substantially improved. Keeping all this in view, the following sectoral strategies are envisaged in the Eleventh Plan for the agriculture and allied activities sector:

- Substantially improve irrigation potential and is utilization.
- Improve water management, rain water harvesting and watershed developments.
- Reclaim degraded land and focus on soil quality.
- Bridge the knowledge gap through effective extension.
- Diversify into high value outputs, fruits, vegetables, flowers, herbs and spices, medicinal plants, bamboo, bio-diesel, etc. but with adequate measures to ensure food security.
- Mixed farming to be encouraged and animal husbandry and fishery activities to be promoted.
- Provide easy access to credit at affordable rates.
- Improve the incentive structure and functioning of markets.
- Refocus on land reforms issues.

Education

Education is an important component of human development. On the Elementary and Secondary education side the ongoing efforts will be continued to achieve hundred per cent enrolment at the Primary and Upper Primary level, reducing the drop-out rate to zero within the shortest possible time span. In the technical and vocational education, focus will be on skill upgradation and ensuring skilled manpower in all trades to meet the emerging requirement of the new industries that are coming up in the state. The state is committed to strive for the realization of the following monitorable targets:

- Reduce drop-out rates of children at the elementary school level to 32 per cent by 2011-12.
- Develop minimum standards of educational attainment in

elementary school and by regular testing monitor effectiveness of education to ensure quality.

- Increase literacy rate for persons of age 7 years or more to 84 per cent.
- Lower gender gap in literacy to 15.1 percentage points.
- Strive to increase the percentage of each cohort going to higher education from the present 10 to 15 per cent by the end of the 11th Plan.

Irrigation and Water Management

The state aims to cover at least 35 per cent of the sown area in each block by assured irrigation during the Eleventh Plan. In order to achieve this objective, each district has been directed to prepare the District Irrigation Master Plan. In the context of the creation of new irrigation potential it will be more effective to provide more funds for the projects for the completion of projects rather than spreading funds thinly for new ones. This way additional potential generation will be quicker. For the flood prone low land of coastal areas effective drainage projects are required to save the crop loss on account of water logging. In this overall scenario the following irrigation and water management measures have been envisaged for the state in the Eleventh Plan:

- Irrigation potential will be increased substantially, with more emphasis on the drought prone areas and watershed development programmes.
- Utilization of irrigation potential created will be stepped up and constantly monitored.
- All the ongoing irrigation projects will be completed on a priority basis.
- Drainage problem to be improved in the waterlogged areas.
- Handing over of irrigation projects to the Pani Panchayat of the water users is being done in the state on a massive scale. This participatory irrigation management process will be continued with greater thrust.
- The innovative participatory Biju Krusak Vikash Yojana (BKVY) of the state will be continued with greater emphasis.

- The policy decision of the State Government for providing irrigation facilities to the extent of 35 per cent of the cultivable area in each block on a priority basis will be continued. The 198 identified blocks having less than 35 per cent irrigated area will be covered and brought above this mark during Eleventh Plan.
- Two mega river basin projects namely, 'Mahanadi Basin Development Plan' and 'Orissa Integrated Irrigation, Agriculture and Water Management Project' are proposed to be taken up during the Eleventh Plan.

Poverty Alleviation and Employment Generation

The state has been making all efforts to substantially reduce poverty both in the rural and urban areas. This will be continued with greater thrust during the Eleventh Plan. Employment generation efforts both for those offering manual labour and also the educated category will be continued during the Eleventh Plan. The following plan strategies will be pursued for the purpose:

- All major ongoing anti-poverty programmes will be continued during the Eleventh Plan.
- All the wage employment generating schemes including NREGS will be continued to be implemented vigorously.
- Continuous efforts will be made to realize the monitorable target of reducing the educated unemployment to below 5 per cent.
- Employment Mission launched during the Tenth Plan will be continued during the Eleventh Plan.
- The state has been pursuing a policy of enhancing the real wage rate of unskilled labourers from time to time for taking care of the effect of inflation. This policy will be continued during the Eleventh Plan.

Public Health and Nutrition

The state is committed to achieve the following monitorable targets set for Eleventh Plan:

- ❖ Reduce Infant Mortality Rate (IMR) to 37 and Maternal Mortality Rate (MMR) to 1.19 per 1000 live births. Also reduce total Fertility Rate to 2.1.
- ❖ Provide clean drinking water for all by 2009 and ensure that there are no slip-backs by the end of the Eleventh Plan.
- ❖ Reduce malnutrition among the children of the age group 0-3 to half its present level and reduce anemia among women and girls by 50 per cent by the end of the Eleventh Plan.

The following plan strategies will be followed to realize the above targets:

- ❖ To provide adequate, qualitative, preventive and curative health care services to the people,
- ❖ To ensure equitable health care services to the disadvantaged groups like the Scheduled Tribes, Scheduled Castes and Other Backward Classes in particular,
- ❖ To provide affordable quality health care to the people not only through the allopathic system of medicine, but also through reliable alternative systems like Ayurveda and Homoeopathy,
- ❖ To ensure greater access to the primary health care facilities by bringing medical institutions close to the people or through Mobile Health Units, particularly in the under-served and backward districts,
- ❖ To improve maternal and child health conditions and to reduce maternal and infant mortality and morbidity rates,
- ❖ To improve hospital services at the secondary and tertiary levels both in terms of infrastructure, personnel and quality of care, and
- ❖ To impart training to the doctors, nurses and other paramedical staff and to upgrade their skills and knowledge to meet needs of health care.

Special Area Development Programmes

The removal of regional disparities has all along been the focus of attention in all the successive Five Year Plans of the state. During the

Eleventh Plan also the issue will get greater focus since the major thrust of the Eleventh Plan, as approved by the NDC, is on broad based inclusive growth. The following initiatives of the Tenth Plan will be continued during the Eleventh Plan with greater emphasis:

- Implementation of the Special Plan for the KBK region.
- Implementation of the Biju KBK Plan.
- Implementation of Programme of the Backward Region Grant Fund.
- Implementation of the Gopabandhu Gramin Yojana.
- Development works in western Orissa through the Western Orissa Development Council.
- Bridging the critical infrastructural gaps in the identified sectors in the TSP areas through grant-in-aid received under Article 275(1) of the Constitution.
- Implementation of development programme in TSP areas with Special Central Assistance funding.

4

Uttar Pradesh

H. C. POKHRIYAL

Given its large population, if Uttar Pradesh does not recover and move more briskly on the development path, the progress of the country as a whole will also get affected. It is critical to India's development strategy that economic growth picks up in Uttar Pradesh at the earliest. Further, if Uttar Pradesh does not do well on Human Development Indices, which are also part of the Millennium Development Goals, India also cannot really hope to meet its international commitment on MDGs or improve its position on the Human Development Index. In the Ninth Plan the growth rate in GSDP (U.P.) was 2.4 per cent and growth rate in GDP (India) was 5.5 per cent (according to 1993-94 base year). In the Tenth Plan, the corresponding figures are 5.3 per cent and 7.7 per cent respectively (according to new series 1999-2000). The per capita income (net state and national income at current prices) according to new series 1999-2000 at the end of the Ninth Plan was Rs. 9781 for U.P. and Rs. 7800 for the nation and at the end of the Tenth Plan the corresponding figures are Rs. 14834 and Rs. 29382 respectively.

Table 4.1 shows that the sectoral composition of NSDP of Uttar Pradesh at current prices in the year 1999-2000 was 38.2, 19.0 and 42.8 per cent of primary, secondary and tertiary sectors respectively, while the corresponding all India figures of GDP were 27.32, 22.99 and 49.69 per cent. Again, in the year 2006-07 as per the advanced estimates, the corresponding figures of Uttar Pradesh were 34.6, 17.6 and 47.8 per cent whereas figures of India for the same year are 20.26,

25.16 and 54.58. From the aforesaid data, the following conclusions can be drawn.

Table 4.1: Percentage Distribution of NSDP at Current Prices of U.P.

Sl. No.	*Year*	*Primary*	*Secondary*	*Tertiary*
1.	1999-2000	38.2	19.0	42.8
2.	2000-01	37.8	17.7	44.5
3.	2001-02	37.1	16.6	46.3
4.	2002-03	36.0	17.5	46.5
5.	2003-04	35.6	17.7	46.7
6.	2004-05	34.5	18.3	47.2
7.	2005-06	34.8	18.2	47.0
8.	2006-07	34.6	17.6	47.8

Table 4.2: Percentage Distribution of GDP at Current Prices of India

Sl. No.	*Year*	*Primary*	*Secondary*	*Tertiary*
1.	1999-2000	27.32	22.99	49.69
2.	2000-01	25.73	23.81	50.46
3.	2001-02	25.47	23.03	51.50
4.	2002-03	23.64	23.65	52.71
5.	2003-04	23.44	23.61	52.95
6.	2004-05	21.75	24.51	53.74
7.	2005-06	21.09	24.85	54.06
8.	2006-07	20.26	25.16	54.58

In Uttar Pradesh, in the year 1999-2000, the share of primary and tertiary sectors was in the neighbourhood of 40 per cent and the share of secondary sector was 19 per cent but in 2006-07 the tertiary sector surged ahead and reached up to 47.8 per cent while the share of secondary sector declined to 17.6 per cent, whereas at the all India level in 1999-2000, the share of the tertiary sector was nearly 50 per cent and the share of primary sector was 28 per cent but in the year 2006-07, the share of the tertiary sector has risen to 54.58 per cent and the share of the primary sector has fallen to 20.26 per cent. This analysis depicts the fact that in Uttar Pradesh the tertiary sector is growing in the same direction as in the country as a whole, but the primary sector is still a dominant sector while at the national level the secondary sector is playing a dominant role.

Year	Per capita income at current prices of Uttar Pradesh (in Rupees)	Per capita income at current prices of India (in Rupees)	Percentage of the UP per capita income against India
1999-2000	9405	15839	59.4
2000-01	9541	16648	57.3
2001-02	9781	17800	54.9
2002-03	10435	18899	55.2
2003-04	11250	20936	53.7
2004-05	11941	22946	52.0
2005-06	13262	25716	51.6
2006-07	14834	29382	50.5

DEVELOPMENT CHALLENGES

Uttar Pradesh is the most populous state of India and the major challenges before the state can briefly be described as:

- Placing the state on high growth trajectory.
- Bridging the increasing gap in the per capita income of the state and India.
- Poverty alleviation.
- Creation of quality infrastructure—roads, power, health, education, irrigation.
- Improvement in the state's ranking in the Human Development Index.
- Positive strides towards the attainment of Millennium Development Goals.
- Improvement in service delivery system.

It is evident from the aforesaid monitorable targets that they are primarily focused on the attainment of a high economic growth rate and improvement on indicators relating to health, nutrition and education among others. It may be noted that on several Health and Nutrition indicators, the position of India, and Uttar Pradesh in particular, is worse than the countries of the Sub-Saharan Africa. Despite posting a growth rate of 9 per cent for the last four years, the position of the country on Human Development Indices has improved only marginally from 127th to 126th position in the World. This is a cause of serious concern and these issues are being targeted in the Eleventh Plan Development strategy.

Table 4.3: Monitorable Targets for the Eleventh Plan

Sl. No.	Indicator	Unit	Present Status		Eleventh Plan Target	
			All India	UP	All India	UP
1.	Infant mortality rate (SRS-2004)	Per thousand	58	72	28	35
2.	Maternal mortality rate (2001-03 RHIMS)	Per lakh live birth	301	517	100	100
3.	Total fertility rate (SRS-2002)	Per productive couple	3.0	4.4	2.1	2.8
4.	Malnutrition of children (0-3 years) (NFHS 1998-99)	Weight for age below 2 SD	47.0	51.7	23.5	23.5
5.	Anemia among women (15-45 years) (NFHS 1998-99)	Percentage	51.8	48.7	25.9	20.0
6.	Sex ratio (0-6 years) (Census 2001)	Per thousand	927	916	935	924
7.	Drop-out in elementary education 2003-04	Percentage	52.22	42.84	20.0	5.0
8.	Literacy rate (Census 2001)	Percentage	64.59	56.23	85.00	85.00
9.	Gender gap in literacy rate (Census 2001)	Percentage	21.6	26.6	10.0	10.0
10.	Additional job needed	In lakhs	—	—	700	125
11.	Poverty ratio (2004-05)	Percentage	27.8	32.2	16.3	15.0
12.	Growth rate	Percentage	7.2	5.6	9.0	10.0
13.	Growth rate in agriculture (primary)	Percentage	1.8	3.5	4.1	6.4
14.	Growth rate in industry (secondary)	Percentage	8.3	6.5	10.5	10.5
15.	Growth rate in services (tertiary)	Percentage	9.0	6.9	9.9	12.4

For the Eleventh Plan, 2007-12, substantial increase in the outlay has been proposed for the priority areas such as Agriculture, Power, Roads, Irrigation, Education, Medical Health and Social net. Similarly, social infrastructure and economic infrastructure have been accorded priority. A brief description is given below.

Item	*Tenth Plan*		*Eleventh Plan Proposed Outlay*		
	Outlay	*Expenditure*	*Total*	*Increase over Tenth Plan Outlay*	*Increase over Tenth Plan Expenditure*
Agriculture and allied activities (including irrigation)	12749.75	10746.76	32270.22	176.6	228.2
Poverty alleviation and employment	6591.51	5282.17	12255.17	85.9	132.0
Power	9082.49	5724.17	26172.28	188.2	357.2
Roads	6008.16	7853.39	24631.09	310.0	213.6
Education	4302.81	5116.64	18736.95	335.5	266.2
Medical Health	2405.43	4133.11	13114.34	445.2	217.3
Water Supply	5337.97	2433.53	5334.92	0.1	119.2
Urban Development	1020.66	1112.53	10847.24	962.8	875.0
Housing	1327.98	1030.13	2807.00	111.4	72.5

PRIORITIES AND THRUST AREAS

The realization of the targeted growth rate of 10 per cent annually, creation of employment opportunities on a massive scale and drastic reduction in poverty appear to be a challenging and tough task. Hence, this needs to be backed up by properly conceived strategies and priorities which may enable one to take care of the weaknesses of the economy on the one hand and help in optimally exploiting the strengths on the other so as to strike a balance between planning and execution. In this context, the objectives and priorities are as follows:

- The plan will focus on and give highest priority to the development of agriculture. To be more precise, it will promote all such activities which increase productivity and motivate farmers to shift from low value to high value crops. The target is to double the income of the farmers during the Eleventh Plan period.

- The development of economic infrastructure, viz. energy, irrigation and transport, will be the second most important objective of the plan and will receive the next highest priority. Development of economic infrastructure is seen as a *sine qua non* for the development of both agriculture and manufacturing sectors, apart from the fact that it provides a base for improvement in the quality of life of the people.
- Measures designed to generate remunerative and productive employment to promote a shift of workforce from agriculture to other sectors of the economy will receive the next highest priority in the plan.
- Provision of universal education, basic health amenities in rural and urban areas, safe and adequate water supply, village connectivity by all weather roads, housing for poor and speedy improvement in the socio-economic conditions of the under-privileged and historically disadvantaged sections of the society will receive a much higher priority in the plan.
- Measures to control growth in population to bring the growth rate at par with that of the country, the programmes initiated for higher literacy, reduction in infant mortality and access to better health care for the poor in rural areas will also receive the highest priority.
- Promoting and developing public-private partnership, the empowerment of the masses and the involvement of self help groups would form part of the strategy.

IMPORTANT GOALS FOR THE ELEVENTH PLAN

The State Government is committed to make Uttar Pradesh a 'prosperous and developed' state where all citizens are able to live in peace and harmony and develop to their full potential without suffering any discrimination based on caste, creed or religion. Inclusive development is the key goal. The State Government has set certain important goals for the Eleventh Plan and these are briefly indicated in the following paras.

State Economy

The State Government has fixed the following general goals for the state:

- Growth rate of at least 10 per cent,
- Reduction in the per capita income gap between the state and the country,
- Improvement in the Human Development Index, and
- Positive steps for the attainment of the Millennium Development Goals.

Farm Sector

Since the farm sector continues to provide employment to about 66 per cent of the population and contributes 34.6 per cent to state's GDP, the State Government has decided to focus attention on agriculture, horticulture, animal husbandry, dairy, fisheries, etc. in a big way. Major goals for the farm sector are as under:

- Double the income of the farmer from that in 2007 by 2012,
- Develop viable 'farm models' for different categories of farms in different agro-climatic zones of the state,
- Ensure easy availability of cheap agricultural credit to farmers,
- Achieve 10 per cent + growth in Dairy, Animal Husbandry, Fisheries and Horticulture sectors,
- Raise surface water irrigation level (canal irrigation) from 21 per cent in 2007 to 33 per cent in 2012,
- Provide adequate funds to the Agriculture Universities and Veterinary Colleges for agriculture and livestock research in the state,
- Reforms in the APMC Act, and
- Provide training and employment to 2 lakh 'Rural Knowledge Workers' through National Council for Cooperative Training (NCCT) during the Eleventh Plan.

Poverty Alleviation

About 32.80 per cent of the state's population are still living below the poverty line. There is urgent need to improve the lot of the poor since almost 20 per cent of the country's poor live in Uttar Pradesh. The following goals have been set in this regard:

- Reduction in poverty from about 32.80 per cent to 15 per cent by the end of the Eleventh Plan,
- Decline in absolute number of poor from about 5.90 crore in 2004-05 to about 3 crore by 2012,
- Improving credit linkage of self help groups from existing 33 to 80 per cent by 2012,
- Establishing federation of all self help groups at the State/ District level, and
- Work for 'financial inclusion' and extend the reach of microfinance in the state to meet credit needs of approximately 80 per cent of the population not directly reached by banks.

Employment Generation

The State Government has fixed a target for the creation of 1.25 crore employments during the Eleventh Plan as it is felt that there is large 'hidden unemployment' in agriculture sector. It is also proposed to focus on improving the 'employability' of workers.

- Credit 1.25 crore employment opportunities during the Eleventh Five Year Plan,
- Imparting of appropriate skills to students as per market requirements after the completion of Basic Education (class VIII, class X and class XII),
- Improve 'employability' of workers, and
- Set up Board of Vocational Education to frame curricula, grant affiliation and conduct test and award certificates to youths trained in vocational skills for both the organized and unorganized sectors.

Human Development Index

The State Government has decided to work towards improving the position of the state on the Human Development Index from its current position wherein the state figures in the 'bottom three' among 15 major states. The goals fixed for education, health and nutrition sectors are as under:

Education

- Achieve full literacy by 2012.
- Gender gap in literacy rate to be reduced from 26.6 per cent in 2001 to 10.0 per cent in 2012.
- Universal enrolment and completion of education up to class VIII by all children.
- Drop-out ratio in Elementary Education to be reduced to 5.0 per cent by 2012.
- Appoint 137000 'Shiksha Sahelis' in all *Anganwadis* to give pre-school education to children in the age group of 3-6 years.
- Computerized tracking of all students studying in class 1 to 8.
- Improving the rank of Uttar Pradesh from the present 29th position among all the states and UTs to among top ten states/ UTs by 2012 on the Education Development Index.

Health and Nutrition

- IMR to be reduced from 72 per 1000 to 35 per 1000 by 2012.
- MMR to be reduced from 517 per 100000 in 2001-03 to 100 per 100000 by 2012.
- Full immunization of children from six deadly diseases.
- Total Fertility Rate to be reduced to 2.8 by 2012.
- Percentage malnutrition among women and children to be reduced to less than 10 per cent by 2012.
- Malnutrition of children below 3 years to be reduced from current level of 51.7 to 23.5 per cent by 2012.
- Anemia among women (15-49 years) to be reduced from the current level of 48.7 to 20.0 per cent by 2012.
- Sex ratio (0-6 years) to be improved from current level of 916 to 924 by 2012.
- Focus on the Public Health-Preventive aspects rather than only on curative aspect.

SOURCE AND SELECT READING LIST

1. *Annual Report* (2005-2006), Ministry of Rural Development, Government of India, New Delhi.

2. *Annual Report* (2006-2007), Department of Agriculture & Cooperation, Ministry of Agriculture, Government of India, New Delhi.
3. *Annual Report* (2006-2007), Ministry of Rural Development, Government of India, New Delhi.
4. *Bihar: Approach to 11th Five Year Plan*—Vision for Accelerated Inclusive Growth, Department of Planning and Development, Government of Bihar, Patna (2006).
5. *Annual Plan* (2006-2007), Department of Planning and Development Department, Government of Bihar, Patna (2006).
6. "Reviving Bihar", editorial, *The Asian Age* (New Delhi: 23-1-2007), p. 6.
7. "All is not Lost for Bihar, Yet", Balmiki Prasad Singh, *The Asian Age* (New Delhi: 10-7-2007), p. 7.
8. Prasad, Yuvaraj Deva and Anil Mishra (ed.), *Rural Development in Bihar: Problems and Prospects*, Har Anand Publications Pvt. Ltd. (New Delhi: 2007).
9. Sachchidananda, K. K. Verma and Manohar Lal, *Social Realities in Bihar*, Novelty & Co. Patna: 1997.
10. Jha, T. N. and K. U. Vishwanathan, *Problems and Prospects of Agricultural development in Bihar*, National Bank for Agriculture and Rural Development, Mumbai: 1999.
11. *Uttar Pradesh Development Report* (Volume 1), Planning Commission, Government of India, New Delhi: Published by: Academic Foundation 4772-73/23, Bharat Ram Road, Darya Ganj, New Delhi-110002 (2007).
12. *Uttar Pradesh Development Report* (Volume 2), Planning Commission, Government of India, New Delhi: Published by: *ibid*.
13. *Economic Survey* (2006-07), Directorate of Economics & Statistics, Planning & Coordination Department, Government of Orissa, Bhubaneswar.
14. *Orissa Development Report*, Planning Commission, Government of India, New Delhi (2002).
15. *Eleventh Five Year Plan: 2007-12 and Annual Plan* (2007-08): Orissa (Volume 1), Government of Orissa, Bhubaneswar (2007).
16. *Annual Plan: 2006-07* (Volume 1), Government of Orissa, Bhubaneswar (2006).
17. *Eleventh Five Year Plan: 2007-12 and Annual Plan* 2007-08: Orissa (Volume 2), Government of Orissa, Bhubaneswar (2007).
18. *Uttar Pradesh: Eleventh Five Year Plan* (2007-2012) and Annual Plan (2007-2008), Volume 1 (Part I), State Planning Commission, Government of Uttar Pradesh, Lucknow (2007).

19. *Uttar Pradesh: Eleventh Five Year Plan (2007-2012) and Annual Plan* (2007-2008), Volume 1 (Part II), State Planning Commission, Government of Uttar Pradesh, Lucknow (2007).
20. *Uttar Pradesh: Eleventh Five Year Plan (2007-2012) and Annual Plan* (2007-2008), Volume II, State Planning Commission, Government of Uttar Pradesh, Lucknow (2007).
21. *Uttar Pradesh: Eleventh Five Year Plan (2007-2012) and Annual Plan* (2007-2008), State Planning Commission, Government of Uttar Pradesh, Lucknow (2007).
22. *Approach to the Eleventh Five Year Plan* for West Bengal, Development and Planning Department, Government of West Bengal, Kolkata.
23. *Annual Plan* (2007-2008): West Bengal, Development and Planning Department, Government of West Bengal, Kolkata.
24. Outlines of Methodology of Gram Sansad Plan Based Gram Panchayat Planning, Department of Panchayat and Rural Development, Government of West Bengal, Kolkata.

EDITOR'S ACKNOWLEDGEMENT

1. Smt. Jaya Dasgupta, IAS, Principal Secretary, Department of Development and Planning, Government of West Bengal, Kolkata.
2. Dr. Manabendra Nath Roy, Principal Secretary, Department of Panchayats and Rural Development, Government of West Bengal, Kolkata.
3. Shri B. P. Shyam Roy, Special Secretary, Department of Development and Planning, Government of West Bengal, Kolkata.
4. Dr. R. V. Singh, IFS, Special Secretary, Department of Planning and Coordination, Government of Orissa, Bhubaneswar.
5. Shri Sanjeev Dubey, IAS, Commissioner and Secretary, Board of Revenue, Uttar Pradesh, Lucknow.
6. Dr. Ajay Kumar Singh, IAS, Director, Land Reforms, Ministry of Rural Development, Government of India, New Delhi.

5

Rural Development
Building a National Perspective

C. ASHOKVARDHAN

Eastern India certainly has the potential for fast growth and development. Its abundant natural and human resources need to be effectively utilized to this end. Concerted effort is especially needed for improvements in the social sector—health and education. It is imperative that the agenda for development in these areas is well conceived keeping in view the needs and aspirations of the people. The present volume analyses the development performance of the economy of the concerning states in the backdrop of socio-ecônomic surveys of villages by the IAS Officer Trainees in various years. The State papers contributed by eminent subject specialists suggest policy highlights wherefrom necessary interventions could follow:

> The strength of the study universe lies in its strong agricultural base and diversified and naturally developed industrial activities across several regions and concentrated tourist centres. Several industrial activities, especially in Uttar Pradesh, are highly export-oriented. However, there are several weaknesses in, and threats to, the progress of Eastern India. For instance, the yield and per capita production of food grain is much lower than other food grain producers in the country, particularly Punjab and Haryana. Low per capita production creates a vicious circle, which needs to be broken

through government interventions. The rural populace badly requires alternative sources of income, which can be provided only through village and urban-based industries and a spurt in the tertiary activities.

Capital in Eastern India is not as productive as it is elsewhere and the states concerned display average levels of industrialization. Hence, promotional strategies need to be worked out in order to transform factory composition and skill levels to increase value addition and at the same time to generate more employment.

The social and physical infrastructure of the region under study is far below the national average in almost every major respect. Access to power, communication, roads and banks critically lag behind other major states in the country. Credit dispersal is lesser than most of the fast growing states. The states studied have lower levels of literacy rate and inadequate institutional development as compared to the national average.

Eastern India lacks in every institutional category—whether in the spread of medical colleges, engineering colleges, universities or research institutes. States such as Andhra Pradesh, Karnataka, Maharashtra, Tamil Nadu, Gujarat, Punjab, are all far ahead of the eastern part of India in one or more categories. Even in middle and secondary level institutions, which are providers of basic education, Uttar Pradesh, for example, has 20 middle and senior secondary schools and 59.54 primary schools per 1,00,000 persons as against the national average of 32 and 65 respectively.

The study universe is threatened by intra-state disparities. Taking a leaf again from Uttar Pradesh, the per capita income in Eastern Uttar Pradesh is half than that in Western Uttar Pradesh. The Central and Bundelkhand regions are also better off than Eastern Uttar Pradesh. However, even the wealthiest part of the state, Western Uttar Pradesh, has a per capita income that is not higher than the national average. Eastern Uttar Pradesh lags in almost all respects: urbanization, investment, industrialization and capital intensity of industrial activity. This calls for special measures to develop the region and remove imbalances within a given state.

Some of the issues vital to rural development are being discussed here in the overall national perspective.

AGRICULTURAL REVIVAL

The growth rate of agriculture in the country was less than two per cent in the last decade. Yield growth has also declined. Farmers' suicides have continued/increased in some states. Farming is becoming a non-viable activity. Further scope for increase in the net sown area is limited. Land degradation in the form of depletion of soil fertility, erosion and water logging has increased. There seems to be a technology fatigue in agriculture. Surface irrigation expansion rate and ground water table have declined. Risk and vulnerability have increased. Disparities in productivity across regions and crops persist.

Globalization policies and the World Trade Organization (WTO) agreements have created many challenges for agriculture like exposure of domestic agriculture to international competition.

Technological upgradation of agriculture is the core element of agricultural development strategy. Technology fatigue occurred because of problems in both research and extension. As a result of extension collapse, the gap between potential and actual yields is quite large in many parts of the country. Although the WTO regime started 12 years back, farmers are still not aware of the implications of globalization and the WTO agreements.

Apart from lower allocations of public investment to agriculture, one of the problem areas is the poor delivery systems is spite of good policies. There is a view that public institutions in agriculture including seed and other input supplies, extension and marketing have collapsed.

Another issue is the political economy of agriculture. There is a feeling that the governments have become less sensitive to the farmers' problems notwithstanding the pro-farmer rhetoric. There are apprehensions that governments are more interested in pleasing the corporate sector (e.g. the SEZ policy) rather than helping the agriculture sector which bears 60 per cent of the burden.

Dependence on Rains

The monsoons define Indian agriculture and, by extension, the Indian economy as well, since more than 60 per cent of the population is still dependent on it for its livelihood and only about 40 per cent of the arable land is under assured irrigation. Apart from the direct impact—agriculture accounts for a little less than 20 per cent of the GDP—

industry is also affected since it provides raw materials for industry and generates demand for industrial goods. The net result is that we have the strange situation of an emerging economic super-power with its fortunes critically dependent on the rains. And since it is not only the quantum but also the spatial distribution and the timing of the rains that is important, it is not enough if the overall precipitation is adequate. Agreed no country can afford to be indifferent to the rains but that is not the same as having a crippling dependence on them. Unfortunately, we have only ourselves to blame for this sorry state of affairs. Over the years, public investment in irrigation has steadily declined. Fortunately, the government has realized its needs to reverse this decline. Irrigation is one of the six components for the development of rural infrastructure under Bharat Nirman and an additional one crore hectare is to be brought under assured irrigation by 2009. Given the deficit, it is a small beginning to be sure, but it marks a welcome re-rating of priorities in agriculture.[1]

The impulse behind the suggestion to substantially hike ground water cess—one among a slew of sensible recommendations on ground water management emanating from a National Advisory Council (NAC) meeting headed by the Union Water Resources Minister is doubtless progressive. But given the fact that ground water is a state subject, the mandatory turn that the NAC has sought to give to its suggestions is no more than high-sounding tokenism. That is, however, not to deny the need for such measures. Proper management of groundwater would not only check its rapid depletion but would help cut power consumption considerably. That would, among other things, help the country earn carbon credits. But groundwater management would have the intended outcome only when it is envisaged as an integral part of an all-party political mission to reform the entire water sector and render it more efficient and equitable. Poor quality and sub-optima levels of water supply, more often than not, fuel extraction of groundwater.

Inequitable access to commons such as water is hardly surprising, given that it is a function of our stratified public realm where a tiny minority of elite corners most of the resources. What has, however, made matters worse is the emergence of a natural resource-intensive industry and modern water-intensive agriculture, with marginal social groups having virtually no say in the matter. The populist government policy of universally subsidizing water supply has further accentuated the problem. Irrationally low water tariffs have prevented utilities from recouping costs for efficient management of our water distribution and sanitation infrastructure. The consequent scarcity and decline in quality has hit the poor, both financially and socially, the hardest. Implementing differential user charges, where per unit tariff goes up with the level of consumption, is one way of eliminating such disparity. Giving people clear water titles, which they would be free to trade or rent out in a free, functional market without fear or favour, must also be put in place. The consensus needed to forge and drive such a political economy can, however, only be created through a larger programme of political action that seeks to transform our hierarchical public realm into a more dialogic and participatory sphere.[2]

Value Additions in Agriculture

The government alone will not be able to implement the value addition strategies in a market led scenario. The corporate sector necessarily has to play a supplementary role to the government's initiatives in the sector. Tax incentives will be a very important tool for incentivising the latter to participate in this sector.

There are three areas which may be considered for immediate deployment of such incentives, amongst others. The first could be in areas in which corporate involvement may have a direct positive effect on the competitiveness of the agri sector, e.g. in providing extension services, farmer's training laboratory facilities for soil testing, residue analysis as well as research and development in areas of seed, crop protection and improved agronomical practices. Second, those related to environment conservation such as water harvesting, wasteland development, etc. where corporates are normally not expected to invest on their own.

Another area may be in the entire spectrum of development of agri-focused infrastructure such as the creation of pre-cooling facilities at farm gates, warehousing and storage infrastructure facilities including cold storage, wholesale/terminal agriculture markets, rural primary as well as *apni mandis*, which are unable to attract enough private investment because of inherent viability gaps, given that the relevant agri eco-systems are not developed as yet to enable a sustainable and independent operation of the businesses. Such tax incentives should be viewed as investments, which will have enormous positive multiplier effects on the agriculture sector and the national economy in general.[3]

Public investment in agriculture since 1990s has declined, which has resulted in poor agricultural performance in recent years. To harness the potential of Indian agriculture, corporate sector is keen to invest in niche areas for organised retailing, processing and exporting through contract farming. Creating a favourable business environment and giving incentives, especially in the rainfed areas, will attract active corporate investment in agri-food sector.

There are enormous untapped opportunities in the rainfed areas, particularly arid and semi-arid tropics, for the production and processing of traditional as well as high-value commodities (especially horticulture and livestock) for raising farm incomes and generating employment opportunities. Experience suggests that corporate investment has responded positively to favourable government policies and improved incentives. Targeting rainfed areas for corporate investment by offering tax exemptions is a welcome move towards reforming the agriculture sector. Such a step will attract corporate investment in rainfed areas to improve access to technology, critical inputs and markets besides ensuring remunerative prices. There are some examples from rainfed areas in high-value food segment, which demonstrate complete transformation of the agrarian economy in selected areas as a result of incentives from the government to the private sector.

Tax concessions to corporate investment would improve the entire value chain and make Indian agriculture more competitive. However, it should be ensured that favourable business environment should not be just for multiplying corporate profits from public goods and incentives. Therefore, the incentives must be linked with institutional reforms to involve farmers in sharing the benefits with the corporate sector.[4]

Private Sector Tie-Up

The Agriculture Produce Marketing Committee (APMC) Act was aimed at keeping food prices low, but it benefits mostly a host of small and inefficient intermediaries while ensuring inadequate returns to the farmer. This factor, in addition to falling expenditures on rural infrastructure, is leading to the decline of Indian agriculture. Reversing this decline will require not just populist sops, but confronting its reasons head on. That will mean at least softening the APMC Act, if not replacing it altogether with a more modern set of regulations that allows agri-business and big retail firms to deal directly and draw up long-term contracts with farmers and their cooperatives. The benefits this would unleash are immense. The private sector would have a stake in investing in agriculture, which would ramp up infrastructure and make available better seeds, extension services, and better know-how to farmers. The enormous wastage of fruits and vegetables that takes place now, to the tune of 35-40 per cent of total produce, would be brought down dramatically. More efficient farming and trading and the security of long term contracts wood boost returns to the farmer.

Intermediate traders and small retailers might lose out initially from such an expansion, but their losses would be off set by the gains of a dynamic agricultural economy. It is up to the Centre as well as state governments to politically manage this transition by ensuring they too get a share of the benefits. But they cannot be allowed to physically restrain organized retail chains from setting up, as happened in Ranchi recently, where a dozen vendors and customers at a Reliance store were hurt and other stores looted by a mob representing vegetable sellers. Even if small traders and local politicians are in sympathy with those who vent their feelings this way, law and order will need to be protected. If certain states should choose to ignore this, they should be bypassed by agribusiness and retail. That would make them fall off the agricultural reform map, and the results would show when disgruntled farmers and consumers compared their plight with counterparts in neighbouring states, where agricultural trade is open to the private sector. There is nothing as powerful as the demonstration effect.[5]

The SEZ (Special Economic Zone) Farm Land Issue

The total cultivable land decreased from 185 million hectares (mh) in 1980 to 183 mh in 2003. During the same period, per capita availability of cultivable land declined from 0.27 mh to 0.18 mh. and non-agricultural use of land increased from 19.66 mh to 24.48 mh. This decrease was mainly due to the diversion of agricultural land for non-agricultural purposes, such as urbanization, roads, industries etc.

Since the SEZ Act came into being, from February 2006 to September 2007, formal approvals have been granted for setting up 362 SEZs. The land area involved is 48,700 hectares, against a cultivable area of 183 million hectares. About 90 approvals were in respect of state industrial development corporation-owned land area of about 21,400 hectares. The highest number of SEZs approved so far have been in Maharashtra, Tamil Nadu and Andhra Pradesh, all with long coastlines of saline soil, as directed by the National Commission on Farmers.

It is sad that the government failed to review the progress on the reclamation of wasteland over the last several years under various central schemes. It has not put a policy in place to ensure that industrial project developers earmark a part of such lands for infrastructure development.

Neither has the government shown enough gravity in focusing on coining a cogent Land Use Policy: not surprisingly, neither the farm ministry nor the rural development ministry—both have officially stated the desire to play a core role in making an efficient National Land Use Policy and the laying down of norms for the formation of Oversight Committees at the state level—have been represented on the board of approval for SEZs.

The farm ministry's own report to the Parliamentary panel stated that prime farmland must be conserved for agriculture and should not be diverted to SEZs. Special programmes should be assigned to wastelands and/or land affected by salinity and other abiotic stresses that reduce the biological potential of land for farming and states should form zoning panels, including soil scientists, to identify non-cultivable land. It is our national interest that agriculture and industry both prosper in a mutually reinforcing manner.[6]

Reforming the Fertiliser Policy

There is ample evidence that large subsidies on fertilizers is not the best way to raise agricultural production. The question from political economy point of view, however, is: how do we make sure that fertilizer subsidy reaches the farmers directly and how do we prune its amount over time and divert the resources saved to investments in agricultural research, and rural infrastructure?[7]

We are faced with an irrational and imbalanced use of fertilizers.

Today the farmers are applying only those fertilizers that are being subsidized by the government: the industry is producing only such fertilizers as are covered under the "subsidy" without giving a serious thought that our soil needs micro nutrients and secondary nutrients along with nitrogen, phosphate and potash to achieve better results.

The government should shift to a nutrient-based subsidy instead of the present product-based subsidy. This would help replenish the required micronutrients and secondary nutrients that have constantly been depleted. A nutrient-based subsidy policy can be introduced using a hybrid model, combining it with direct assistance to small and marginal farmers. The government can decide about the mode of disbursement of subsidy to farmers directly or any other suitable mode, but manufactures should be given freedom to produce various products and sell them at reasonable rates.

Shifting from naphtha to natural gas shall make a significant saving to the government. At our Phulpur Unit alone with a change of feed stock from naphtha to gas, a saving to the tune of Rs. 1,000 crore per annum has been achieved. If all the fertiliser companies using naphtha shift to natural gas, there shall be a substantial saving.[8]

The expenditure of Rs. 17,000 crore in the year 2006-07 and the expenditure of Rs. 28,000 crore in the year 2007-08 on account of fertiliser subsidy are big amount but the amount for the year 2008-09 is likely to be bigger, given the fact that the prices of feedstock will continue to rise and the efficiency in the fertilizers industry is not expected to improve, in any case. Given this, the fertilizer subsidy estimate in the coming 2008-09 budget would be somewhere around Rs. 40,000 crore, if not more.

The sum of Rs. 40,000 crore as fertiliser subsidy, even though much of it does not reach the farmers at all, is only a fraction of the negative subsidy imposed by the government on the farmers by way of depressed prices of agricultural produce for many decades. On that count the subsidy appears justified.

However, a nutrient-based subsidy is required to be considered not from the point of view of controlling the burden of the subsidy. The review is more important because the current subsidy policy, so far, had a tilt towards urea (nitrogen) with the result that nitrogen is being over-used while there is a deficiency in the use of Phosphate (P) and Potash (K). The lopsided nutrient use has already had a bad effect and will affect the Indian agriculture very adversely in the years to come. As to the feedstock, the question is not whether the industry uses naphtha or natural gas, the more important question is what are going to be the trends in the prices of the feedstocks.[9]

Future's Markets

Future's markets allow free interaction among players who bring available information related to current and projected demand and supply, weather forecasts, crop size estimates, yield, substitutes position, tariff and tax policies, etc. and thereby help in fair and efficient price determination. Futures markets also help in hedging the price risk. The information should be allowed to enter public domain *via* markets else the information holders may use it to manipulate the market. When transparency is missing the traders make a killing and the farmer loses. The government too loses in terms of high import price. Early price signals can help plan suitable trade policies and time exports and imports. Exporters can hedge against price risk in proposed purchases in the physical market to fulfil export commitments and importers can hedge against possible competition from a potential fall in the prices of imports. This would improve import-export competitiveness.

Even if futures markets are not fully efficient they would still provide some signals to determine quantity, price and timing of exports and imports. The processors too can hedge against price fluctuations in agri-inputs. A fair market price to the farmer would reduce government responsibility of providing subsidized inputs and price support for output. The money can be used in the creation of the much-needed agricultural infrastructure. The futures price information would help farmers take critical sowing decisions instead of being dependent on MSP, which being administered may provide signals out of sync with market realities. Studies by IIM, Lucknow and NCDEX have shown that futures markets generally benefit farmers through higher prices.

There is a need to encourage small farmers to link-up with futures market through instruments such as mutual funds, allowing aggregators to bid on their behalf. However, even if farmers are unable to participate in the futures market, the mere availability of futures price would significantly reduce manipulation/fluctuation in the spot markets and curb arbitration across *mandis*. Improved price predictability would ensure that agriculture delivers in sync with market forces of demand and supply, thus improving our agricultural competitiveness. The Ware House Development Bill (passed by Parliament) along with futures market can go a long way in increasing the holding power of our farmers and enable them to time their sales. There would be increased investment in warehouse development, grading and standardization of produce.

This would induce farmers to improve product quality to a level acceptable to exchanges and hence the market, thus raising their returns. Futures market along with tradeable warehouse receipt would also help farmers improve credit accessibility.[10]

Organic Agriculture

Organic agriculture holds the key for rural transformation and sustainable development in our country. This practice of agriculture involves preservation of natural bio-diversity and effective management of biological and natural resources to improve farm productivity and pest management without the use of any external inputs such as chemical fertilisers, chemical pesticides, and genetically modified inputs. With organic farming practices, the country will be less dependent on unsustainable inputs, which would simultaneously enhance local environmental resources and national food security, while contributing towards rural livelihood opportunities.

Though there are obvious benefits of organic cultivation and consumption, the small and marginal farmers face a challenge to guarantee their produce as organic in local and domestic markets.

The third-party certification process to guarantee organic produce involves exhaustive documentation and high costs which are beyond the capacity of the small farmers. As an alternative, a community based certification with local standards has been pioneered by Dr. Alexander Daniel of the Institute for Integrated Rural Development, Aurangabad and implemented in Paithan Taluka of Maharashtra since 1998.[11]

Agro-Chemicals

Considering the fact that India does not have any particular advantages with regard to petroleum feed stocks and the future scenario is likely to become more difficult, alternative plans have to be thought of at the national level to sustain the overall growth in the chemical industry.

The country is missing the opportunities in the agro-chemical sector, which can provide multiple benefits and opportunities for sustained growth.

There are a number of agro-chemicals that have huge potential but remain unexploited in the country. Many such agro-chemicals can be potential substitutes for petrochemicals with several advantages. Such agro-chemicals can provide ecological and environmental advantages, as they are largely biodegradable and most of them do not have any side effects.

Of course, the first agro chemical that would come to anybody's mind is starch. The most promising product out of starch is lactic acid/poly lactic acid that provides enormous opportunities to substitute petro-based conventional plastic material. Poly lactic acid is biodegradable and provides ecological advantages. Cargill is the pioneer in the field of poly lactic acid in the world and has now set up a project capacity of 140,000 tonnes per annum in the US. Several other global organizations are considering similar projects not only for poly lactic acid but also other nature-based biodegradable plastics.

In view of the environmental compulsions to replace synthetic petro-based plastics, the global demand for biodegradable plastic is likely to increase steadily at the rate of not less than 15 to 20 per cent per annum in the next decade. In the field of biodegradable plastics, India has no significant presence in the global market and any worthwhile research and development efforts in tune with the global development are yet to be initiated in the country.

There are many other starch based derivatives such as citric acid, L-lysine, glutamic acid/monosodium glutamate, etc., which can be produced in large quantity. But the country at the moment has little or no presence in such areas.

Another exciting area is the range of castor-based products. Even with India remaining as the largest producer of castor seeds in the world, many castor-based products such as sebasic acid are not adequately produced in the country. On the other hand, China has a large presence in such castor-based products, whereas India still remains a large exporter of castor seeds/castor oil, without converting them into more profitable value-added products.[12]

The Ethanol Programme

The ethanol programme is farmer-friendly and tailor-made for India given that 72.2 per cent of the Indian population lives in rural areas and agriculture accounts for 20 per cent of the country's GDP. It is also an energy security programme—the country meets 70 per cent of its crude oil requirements through imports. Ethanol is also an environment-friendly fuel, as it reduces the emission of harmful green house gases.

Critics say that the ethanol programme may be actually creating a food shortage. But not in India. In the US ethanol is made from corn. Brazil makes it directly from the sugarcane juice. But India makes ethanol from molasses, a by-product of sugar manufacturing. India's sugar production was 30 million tonnes in 2006-07, as against 20 million tonnes in 2005-06. This has augmented the availability of molasses, enough to yield 1.100 million litres of additional alcohol, which is sufficient for a 10 per cent ethanol programme. Moreover, sugarcane is cultivated on 5.16 million hectares—just 2.3 per cent of total gross cropped area of the country.

Another fear is that of sustainability of supplies. The ethanol programme disruption in 2004-05 is often offered as an argument. Sugar production had fallen due to poor monsoon in two consecutive years Maharashtra. But that was an exception. A long-term programme cannot hinge on the weather. The concern over the shortage of distillation capacity is unfounded as capacity utilization is only 60 per cent for lack of demand. In UP, the largest sugar producer, against the installed annual capacity of 1,260 million litres production is 800 million litres. The state already caters to the 5 per cent ethanol programme. Once 10 per cent ethanol is mandated, operating distilleries may enhance output and those shut may restart. Besides, there will also be supplies from distilleries coming up in the new integrated sugar complexes. Twenty-four new distilleries have got environmental clearance. This means 435 million litres of additional alcohol. The energy argument does not hold. Energy from bagasse exceeds the energy required to produce sugar and alcohol by 0.25 Gcal per tonne of sugarcane crushed. In balance, the ethanol programme will do a world of good to India.[13]

Pivotal Role of Agriculture in Rural Development

Indian agriculture needs to catch up with a 4 per cent annual growth and only value addition can bring about dramatic improvements in the farm sector and result in higher incomes at different points of the rural economy. The complex nature and structure of the Indian agrarian economy with highly fragmented land holdings and, subsistence and marginal farming, inadequate levels of technology, credit and marketing linkages makes it difficult to deploy any initiative in the agri-value chains. Therefore, only a demand driven agricultural development strategy can make the desired impact on the agri-value chains leading to higher-farm incomes.

According to government data, 127 million cultivators and 107 million farm labourers depend on the farm income. The diversion of 1,000 hectares of cultivable land for non-farm purposes would deprive about 900 cultivators and 760 labourers of livelihoods. The key concern, though, is food security and crop productivity. We would be short of some 25 million tonnes of food grain by 2010-11 (presuming a desirability of 256 million tonnes of food grain by 2010-11), with the present growth of production persisting. By that time, the projected food production growth rate has to be at least 3.2 per cent to meet the production target for a population that should only be growing at 1.6 per cent.

Meeting the nutritional requirement of the population with declining arable land will be an uphill task that calls for concerted awareness campaigns at all social levels. Agriculture will remain the mainstay of global economics as long as people need food to survive, more so in developing countries such as rural-heavy India. Unless this sector's genuine concerns are addressed on priority basis, the hollowness of such plan would be exposed.

India has several advantages with regard to agro sector like vast land area, different climatic zones, various soil conditions, etc. What is needed is a comprehensive and pragmatic agro plan to develop and cultivate various crops, under the national planning scheme, which can pave the way for the production of various value-added agro-chemicals.

Today, unfortunately, there is no national agro plan as such in the country with regard to the extent of area firmly allotted for different crops and the targeted production level. It is left to the farmers to decide as to what they would cultivate and the farming community generally takes community decision largely based on local consultative process. The choice of crops for cultivation is always decided at the local level without the government having any control over the matter.

Ensuring well functioning markets, facilitating competition, creating an enabling environment for direct producer-buyer linkages and institution building for farmers provide some recent examples of success in the agricultural landscape. When added to the traditional approach of risk management in the form of moisture conservation, irrigation and technology transfer, there appears fresh hope on the farm front. At the policy level the challenge before the state agencies is to respond to the dynamism displayed by the farmers with matching changes in the regulatory framework. It is policy which is lagging in sufficient flexibility to reduce controls further and create greater space for innovative risk management devices to emerge.[14]

HEALTH AND NUTRITION CONCERNS

Basic Health Indicators

Every year, 400,000 people in India die of T.B. For India's growth and democratic dividend to have any meaning, the government must step up funds for health, focus on delivery systems and, importantly, invite the private sector to invest in health. With the country growing at 9 per cent and the tax to GDP ratio improving in recent years, the time is ripe to effect a policy shift.

For a nation on the move, its basic health indicators are grim. Life expectancy at birth, at 64 years, is more or less on a par with Pakistan and Bangladesh, while the Sri Lankans and the Chinese can expect to live till they are 74. Infant mortality is 54 per 1,000 live births, against 23 and 19 in the case of China and Sri Lanka, respectively. India's maternal mortality rate, at 301 per 100,000 live births, is terrible when compared to 92 in the case of Sri Lanka. The National Family Health Survey-3 tells us that 46 per cent of young children in India are under-weight, compared to 6 per cent in China and 31 per cent in Pakistan. An Indian cannot be expected to be healthy after 54, whereas an average Chinese is healthy till he turns 65.

Centre and state spending on health accounts for just 1.39 per cent of the gross domestic product, or about Rs. 57,000 crore. In contrast, education gets a better deal, with Centre and state spending accounting for 2.87 per cent of GDP. There is no reason why health should not be treated on par with education. The two sectors should be developed in tandem. Midday meals must be an integral part of the Sarva Shiksha Abhiyan while medicine should form the central thrust of the government's higher education budget with a need to addressing the shortage of doctors and nurses. Pre-natal and post-natal programmes as well as the nutritional needs of children below five deserve special emphasis.

More funds alone will not do the trick. The government should improve delivery systems as it has done in the case of education and recast its budget to concentrate on a clutch of key areas, while leaving the rest to private enterprise. Private players must weigh in strongly in the areas of hospitals and health insurance, so that access to health services improves. Just as poor health acts as a drag on productivity, a healthier population will spur growth to even more dizzying heights.[15]

Maternal Mortality

Data on maternal mortality in India show that tens of thousands of malnourished, health-poor and resource-poor women without access to hospitals continue to die during pregnancy, while giving birth or immediately afterwards. Maternal Mortality Ratio (MMR) is an important indicator of the reach of clinical health services to the poor, and a composite measure of the overall quality of life. The MMR has no doubt dropped significantly in recent decades. It fell to 301 (per 100,000 live births) in 2001-03, from 398 in 1997-98. The figure was as high as 750 in the 1960s. While this is quite an achievement for India which used to rank high globally in maternal mortality, the pace of decline is not enough. About 78,000 women continue to die here each year. This is a significant proportion of a total of five lakh pregnancy-related deaths globally. The U.N. Millennium Development Goal is to bring the MMR down to 200 by 2007, and to 109 by 2015.

The crisis is rooted in poverty and social iniquity. India continues to spend a lower percentage of GDP—2.4 per cent—on public health compared virtually to every other country. The scale of the tragedy can be reduced by stepping up interventional strategies and facilitating institutional delivery. In 2003, only about 28 per cent of all births in India took place in institutions. Two-thirds of the deaths occurred in the northern swathe that includes Rajasthan, Uttar Pradesh/ Uttaranchal, Madhya Pradesh/Chhattisgarh, Bihar/Jharkhand, and

Orissa, as well as Assam. Significantly, only 15.8 per cent of births occurred in institutions in these states, as against the all-India figure of 28.3 per cent on the other hand, in the four southern states, which account for 18 per cent of the births, 64 per cent were institutional, explaining their much better performance in this area. The correlation is hard to miss. A massive and time-bound programme to increase institutional delivery in the low performing states can make a real difference. The government should devise a composite package to improve institutional infrastructure in the area of maternal health, and provide quick and easy access to round-the-clock emergency obstetric care everywhere. A broader blood safety agenda needs to be pursued, aimed at providing universal access to safe blood transfusions. For, excessive blood loss accounts for a quarter of all deaths related to child-birth. At a fundamental level, the nutritional and health status of women needs to be improved, especially in the rural areas. It is time the special health care needs of motherhood were given urgent attention.[16]

Child Malnutrition

Estimates for India reveal that 20 to 30 per cent of babies weigh less than 2,500 grams at birth. This suggests the onset of malnutrition in the womb itself and reflects an inter-generational transfer of malnutrition from the mother to the child. Adversely affecting the birth of well-nourished babies is also the poor health and nutritional status of women.

The second factor has to do with the limited reach of the public health services and messages. In 2005-06, for instance, only 44 per cent of children of age 12 to 23 months were fully immunized. And only 26 per cent of children with diarrhoea were given oral rehydration salts. Barely two-thirds (64%) of children suffering from acute respiratory infection or fever were taken to a health facility. Also affecting the health and nutritional well-being of children is the limited reach of, and access to, maternal care services. Here again, NFHS-3 reveals some glaring shortfalls. In 2005-06, barely half (51%) of mothers across the country received at least three antenatal care visits during pregnancy, and less than half 48 per cent of births are attended to by a trained birth attendant, which includes a doctor, nurse, woman health worker, auxiliary nurse and midwife, and other health personnel.

The third clue lies in the case of the child. Breast milk provides vital nutrients throughout the first year of life; but this alone is not sufficient. Beyond four to six months, infants must be given solid foods to supplement breast milk. Despite the importance of breastfeeding and appropriate feeding for preventing malnutrition, only 23 per cent of children under the age of three were breastfed within one hour of birth and less than half the babies (46%) up to five months old were exclusively breastfed. And only 56 per cent of children aged six to nine months received solid or semi-solid food and breast milk. It is, therefore, not surprising that a child typically becomes malnourished between six and 18 months of age, and remains so thereafter. In most cases, nutritional rehabilitation is difficult.

And the fourth clue is found in the limited opportunities available to women. Access to education, for instance, makes a big difference. According to NFHS-3, malnutrition among the Indian children below the age of three born to illiterate mothers (55%) is more than twice the levels (26%) reported among mothers who have completed more than 10 years of schooling.

There are three important issues relating to the care of the child. First, six-month babies cannot feed by themselves, they need to be fed small amounts of food frequently. Feeding a six-month-old infant, however, is time-consuming. Many rural women simply do not have the luxury of time to feed infants. The task is often entrusted to an older sibling who understandably may not have the required patience to feed an infant. Related to this is the need to care for pregnant women by ensuring proper nutritional diet and by reducing the burden of work on mothers. Child rearing in most families is made the primary responsibility of others. It is important for fathers too to recognize their role in child care and share the burden with mothers. And third, it is important for state interventions to focus on the care of newborns and those under the age of three.

Levels of child malnutrition in India are exceptionally high. According to the recently released National Family Health Survey, NFHS-3, carried out in 2005-06, 46 per cent of India's children under the age of three are underweight. The corresponding levels of child malnutrition are much lower in most other countries—28 per cent in Sub-Saharan Africa and eight per cent in China. Scientific evidence suggests that compared with the risks a well nourished child faces, the risk of death from common childhood diseases is doubled for a mildly malnourished child, tripled for a moderately malnourished child, and may be even as high as eight times for a severely malnourished child.[17]

In a country where the stock market has crossed 17,000 points, where inflation is under control, where the economic growth rate is climbing, almost one in every two children under three years of age is hungry. This is the invisible half of our population, people who disappear from our consciousness until they die in large numbers. Then, the media wakes up and takes note, the incident becomes a "breaking news", the government squirms when though questions are asked, some remedial measures are put into place, and soon life reverts to "normal", or, should we say, abnormal.[18]

The public sector health needs to be re-crafted with a thrust on community ownership for autonomous hospitals, flexible financing for local decision-making, innovation in human resource engagement for service guarantees, monitoring against public health standards, and building capacities at all levels. The National Rural Health Mission is one such concerted effort at crafting a credible public system.

Such crafting would be effective only when it ensures the availability of well-skilled health workers, who have the resources to meet people's health needs. The public sector needs a large-scale expansion of community health workers, nurses and para-medics at all levels to take care of the primary health needs. More medical officers and specialists are also needed to provide appropriated referral lands at all levels. That does not mean there is no scope for partnerships with non-governmental providers for public health goals. Accreditation of private providers through transparent criteria and engagement of private professionals on a case-to-case basis are ways of taking the partnership forward, more so given the shortage of doctors in the rural healthcare public system.[19]

All over the traditional western oriented healthcare system, with its strong emphasis on hospital care and curative approach, is proving to be much too expensive. Rapid changes in the disease pattern, and rapid urbanization, have led to an 'epidemiological transition' in developing countries like India, where deaths from non-communicable diseases such as cardiovascular, cerebrovascular diseases, cancer and diabetes have seen an unprecedented rise. The curative approach based on an estimated 80 per cent infectious and 20 per cent non-infectious diseases now appears skewed. It is time to consider a preventive model.

This would need a re-engineering of our healthcare delivery system. The aim must not only be to make healthcare affordable and accessible to all segments of our society, but to remodel to a wellness based one. We need to start addressing the erosion of the linkages that are self-evident in public health—health and sanitation, increasing health and sanitation, increasing health awareness, availability of safe drinking water, and nutrition. We parallely need to fight, with information and innovation, the root causes of cardio-vascular, cancer and diabetes.[20]

The government has been pushing for a rural Healthcare Plan arguing that the healthcare delivery capability is concentrated in urban areas.

The need of the hour is to develop a model that is not only suitable for India and its large population but at the same time commercially viable for investors to put in their money. Certain state governments and private entities are experimenting with a micro insurance model. These models can work, provided there are innovative solutions and a partnership between the public and private sector.

A generic outline for one such programme can be that the Indian government puts aside a sum of Rs. 5,000 crore as a corpus to encourage micro insurance schemes from its total annual healthcare outlay of Rs. 20,000 crore. Patients would then be able to decide which hospitals they want to go to. The government could formulate a policy, which would allow patients to choose from a list of approved hospitals as per specific needs. Simplifying the math, if the government buys Rs. 100 premium per person and puts Rs. 5,000 crore into the corpus, it could cover 50 crore people. Going by the volume of business, we should be able to get a Rs. 1 lakh insurance cover for people under the scheme.

In a country where the majority of the population lives in rural areas, tools like telemedicine can contribute substantially in bridging the gap between the demand and supply of healthcare services, especially in the far-flung areas. Using this technology, patients could be examined, monitored and treated, virtually without necessarily having the immediate physical presence of a doctor. The Fortis Foundation and Khushi (NGO) partnership at Neemrana, in

Rajasthan, is one such successful programme that has been well received by the people of the area.

There are also winning models of private health insurance schemes like the one started by the renowned Dr. Devi Shetty who runs the Narayana Hrudayalaya Hospital. His Yashaswini Health Insurance Scheme provides coverage to two million farmers at a meagre and very affordable premium of around Rs. 10 per month. It includes around 300 private and government hospitals from all over Karnataka. The success of this scheme has inspired similar initiatives in other states.[21]

EDUCATION REFORMS

Compared to the below 20 per cent literacy rate in 1950, the present percentage of around 68 is certainly a great advancement, particularly against several odds and a three-fold increase in population. Prestigious institutions of engineering, technology, management and research have come up and several of these have achieved credibility at the highest levels internationally. The education system can claim credit for the recognition achieved by India internationally. India now has an economic growth rate of over 9 per cent. This has to be sustained by a young manpower well-versed in skills and fully competent to respond to the emerging demands in the labour market.

Though an impressive increase in the number of schools and institutions has taken place, the school drop-out rate for the age group 6-11 years was 30 per cent in 2001, and 29 in 2004. In the 21st century this is an abnormally high percentage. The pressure on the system to expand and extend its outreach at each stage is on the increase. In terms of content and pedagogy, fast-paced introduction of the new techniques emerging as a consequence of developments in IT and ICT are being incorporated and integrated. This requires a far greater emphasis on training, retraining and in-service education of teachers, academics and researchers.

The flagship schemes of the Human Resource Development Ministry (MHRD) like SSA and Mid-day meal have just achieved numbers to project as progress without much emphasis on quality and learner achievement. The expansion in secondary education has not kept pace with the growing demand for vocational and technical courses in emerging areas. At present, the gross enrolment ratio at the secondary stage stands at 51.65. The government intends to take it to 75 by the end of the Eleventh Plan in 2012. This would require an additional enrolment of 90.3 lakhs. The system would need 6.5 lakh more teachers, apart from other infrastructure inputs. These initiatives which are a must, have been delayed by a couple of decades.

At the secondary stage, the major issue, however, is the introduction of vocational and technical education courses. Further, it is also a tough task to generate awareness among the youngsters and their families that successful completion of Technical and Vocational Education and Training (TVET) could open larger and attractive avenues. There are also related issues of placement, equivalence, upward mobility and reorientation. At the secondary stage, access to education for girls living in remote, hilly or tribal areas is also a major concern.[22]

The Outsourcing Boom

The outsourcing boom of the 21st century has transformed India. From a developing country, we are today an emerging economy and a superpower in the making. Over the last few years, India has moved up the offshoring value chain—from being a low-cost destination to a knowledge hub to the world. Today, 5.2 per cent of the country's GDP comes from export of IT and IT-enabled services (ITES).

Every year, 3,00,000 engineering graduates and approximately two million graduates pass out of colleges. But only 10-15 per cent of the graduates are suitable for employment in offshore IT and BPO industries. Nearly two-thirds of the 3,00,000 engineering graduates need to be reskilled, so that they can get jobs in the IT industry.

Even those who find jobs need to undergo training and be reskilled. Today, India needs to skill/reskill one million working executives. Emerging sectors such as retail, banking, financial services and insurance (BFSI) industries are facing an acute shortage of manpower. The banking industry, which employs 9,00,000 people, is expected to add 6,00,000 more over the next five years. But it is unclear how this increased demand will be met.

The shortage of skilled talent threatens to slowdown the Indian IT and ITES industry if the education system does not keep pace with the rising talent needs. As per estimates, by 2010, the industry will need approximately 8,50,000 additional skilled manpower.

Meanwhile, the developed world requires fuel of another kind—knowledge workers and skilled professionals. By 2000, the developed world will have a shortage of 40 million working people, says a report—India's New Opportunity 2020—brought out by the All India Management Association, the Boston Consulting Group and the Confederation of Indian Industry.

A recent study by global HR consultancy Manpower Inc says that 41 per cent of employers world-wide are having difficulty in filling positions due to lack of suitable talents in their markets.

For the developed world, this is a serious matter. Manpower shortages can cripple economic growth. It can escalate wage rates, thereby reducing the competitiveness of these countries. Blessed with surplus workforce, countries like India and China can meet the manpower shortages of the developed world.

This is where India requires substantial public private partnerships. NIIT is undertaking initiatives to generate skilled manpower resources in small towns and villages. In August 2007, NIIT inaugurated its first model district learning centre (DLC) at Chhindwara in Madhya Pradesh. The DLC is geared towards fostering talent and skilled manpower resources for global readiness. Over 4,000 students graduate every year from the Chhindwara district.

The DLC will provide intensive training programmes to over 200 students a year. It will work towards increasing the capacity by another 200 students in the next two years. Once the model is tested, NIIT plans to roll out similar initiatives in other districts of the country. These graduates will be equipped with various skills, such as IT, communication (verbal and written), and business etiquette that will enable them to acquire gainful employment.[23]

Science Education in Schools

Attempts to challenge the orthodoxy of the Indian science education have mostly been very small in scale. An exception is the Hoshangabad Science Teaching Programme (HSTP), a programme for teaching middle school science through experiments, which started in 1972 as a pilot project in 16 schools of Hoshangabad district in Madhya Pradesh. At the time of its abrupt closure in 2002, it was running around 1000 schools in 16 districts of the State. The HSTP was unique in, that it was a State Programme, running the programme in ordinary

Government schools, supported by a large academic resource group. Although no longer a running programme, the HSTP has had great influence on the discourse on education in the country.

An important difference between the HSTP and the conventional science teaching is that the former emphasised the processes of science-observation, recording, performing controlled experiments, etc. On the other hand, conventional school science emphasised the "Products" of science—laws, theories etc. In some sense the process-product debate continues to this day, with the mainstream in favour of teaching products.

Science should emerge as something alive, fallible, and therefore exciting. Such a model will meet the wider aims of science education, and at the same time is more likely to encourage potential scientists to want to study science.

NCERT, in its National Curriculum Framework document of 2005, addresses the issue afresh. The "Product" obsession of school science is acknowledged. For the first time, HSTP and other similar efforts find place in a major policy document. Moving towards a curriculum that is less laden with facts, weakening disciplinary boundaries and linking school knowledge with outside knowledge are its avowed goals.[24]

Teachers' Training

In recent times, significant advancements have been made in understanding how children grow. Several researches have been conducted on child behaviour. The findings of these researches generally do not reach the teachers in the language that they will understand. Dynamic systems of education utilize these new findings to find how children learn from various sectors like medical sciences, psychology, pedagogical sciences and so on. The results of these researches should be made part of the training imparted in teacher training institutes and in school classrooms.

It is a fact that teachers are facing problems when meeting the new expectations that the system has of them. The fact that they face psychological stress cannot be ignored. That some teachers' behaviour borders on the unacceptable is often because of work pressure, especially when schools do not have enough teachers. Then they are assigned non-professional tasks, and are made to perform conflicting roles. Essentially, there is an inherent conflict when school teachers have to combine teaching and disciplining their students with dealing with parents and the community. It is only when there are effective teacher preparation programmes in good institutes that these teachers will be able to strike a balance between these roles.[25]

Neglecting teacher training has further compounded the losses incurred on account of indifferently induced, or entirely absent, curricular changes. Teachers constitute the most important factor in determining the quality of children's experience at school. Today, millions of children born to illiterate parents are expected to attend school, yielding the exciting potential to nurture a thoughtful and tolerant society of the kind the Constitution envisions. Yet hardly any state is in a position to realize this potential because the welfare and training of teachers have been ignored everywhere. Instead of moving forward in this sector we have actually regressed. School teachers had played an important role in the national movement, both as individuals and as a professional group. Far from treating them as a national resource, Independent India treated them as a faceless mass of literate workers. The Chattopadhyaya Commission appointed by Smt. Indira Gandhi in 1983 noted that "today the average teacher's perception of his role and responsibility is far too limited and is concerned with his own immediate tasks." The Commission felt that the teacher must "actively and feelingly associate himself, as an essential and responsible partner, in the great tasks which face the nation." This recommendation failed to save the school teacher's status as it declined rapidly over the decade of the 1990s, and continues to do so today. The profession has lost all attraction for the young, due to which only those who fail to materialize all other aspirations accept teaching as a last resort.[26]

ECONOMIC REFORMS AND POVERTY

India has benefited by opening up its economy. The downside of the globalization of Indian economy is that it has lowered the incomes of the poorest in the country. Like, for example, cotton farmers, who found themselves unable to compete in the global marketplace thanks to the subsidies enjoyed by farmers elsewhere. That is probably one of the major reasons for the suicide by cotton farmers in India.[27]

If economic reforms have created a new world that simply did not exist earlier, they have also created aspirations that were unheard of 15 years ago. And that is the real challenge. The post-reform period has seen one of the fastest periods of reduction in poverty, but there is no doubt that in absolute numbers we are still home to one-third of the world's poor. The ground has been laid. There is a new dynamism created by the record 8 per cent plus GDP growth for four consecutive years. This could provide a launching pad for even higher growth in the years to come, provided we use the opportunity wisely. Reform is about changing mindsets, but it is even more about effecting that change within a reasonable timeframe. The reason is simple: the world will not wait while we debate endlessly about pension reform, increasing foreign direct investment (FDI) in insurance, allowing FDI in retail, raising the voting cap in banks so that board decisions reflect shareholding, and so on. The growing tide of red, as seen in the spread of Naxalite movement across large swathes of the country, is a telling and chilling reminder of the fact that some of our countrymen have run out of patience. They are not prepared to wait indefinitely for reform to touch their lives. The agenda of reform 'waiting to be taken up', is well known. It will not brook any further delay.[28]

While the growth rate of the economy is impressive, there is a need for a course correction to ensure that the rural sectors do not get excluded. We have to see how the rural people relate to growth.

We have to see how to bring them into the mainstream by providing adequate employment opportunities.

The report of the National Commission for Enterprise in the Unorganised Sector (NCEUS) goes to show that reforms have been a qualified success in a benchmark of Rs. 11.60 per person per day (the minimum amount of calories required to sustain an individual, expressed in money terms) to estimate the proportion of people earning below Rs. 20.30 per person per day as well. Going by household expenditure data of the National Sample Survey Organization (NSSO), 22 per cent of the population exists below the poverty line. But what is less known is that the proportion of the population earning between Rs. 11.60 and Rs. 15 per person per day is 19 per cent and between Rs. 15 and Rs. 20 per person per day 36 per cent. In other words, 55 per cent of India live on Rs. 12.30 per capita per day. The report calls them 'vulnerable'. While the percentage of population below the poverty line has fallen in the reform years, the movement has broadly been from the poor to this 'vulnerable' category.

An average growth rate of about 6.5 per cent in the post-reform years has cut into poverty. Thirty one per cent of the population was below the poverty line in 1993-94, against 26 per cent in 1999-2000 and 22 per cent in 2004-05. Those in the next category, living on about Rs. 15 a day, have remained virtually the same at about 19 per cent over this decade.

The proportion of the middle-income category, living on about Rs. 37 per capita per day, has risen from 15.5 to 19.3 per cent. The high-income category, living on four times the per capita income, or about Rs. 93 per person, is up from 2.7 per cent of the population to 4 per cent. The per capita expenditure of the average Indian is Rs. 23 per day. Poverty has fallen by nine percentage points between 1993-94 and 2004-05, about the same in the 1980s.[29]

Today, we need an Indian consensus and commitment that our economic growth is both inclusive and sustainable. Innovative, locally relevant approaches that can enhance the capacity of the underprivileged people in both the urban and rural areas to access the emerging economic opportunities, and to shield themselves from the increased economic risk are necessary.

Fundamental changes are needed in the way we design and deliver programmes like credit, information, health, education, infrastructure and rural economic diversification, and how government partners with others. Fortunately, a great deal of experimentation has been taking place at the micro-level-involving innovative government officials, enlightened business, banks, NGOs, and others.

A distinctive Indian capitalism is emerging, but it is difficult to discern its outlines. The pace of economic and social change is faster than ever. How humane will this capitalism be? Today, our market-oriented ethos seems individualistic and myopic. Do we have the ability to recognize that our collective self-interest lies in urgently creating a system where the potential benefits of national and international markets can come within the reach of all citizens?[30]

Reforms have delivered higher and sustained growth, and growth has made a dent on poverty. The pace of reduction of poverty is, however, roughly the same in the pre- and post-reform decade. Percentage reduction in poverty is much harder now, and hence 36 to 26 is much more impressive than 46 to 36 in the pre-reform decade. Today's poverty rate is half of 1951, but since population is more than three times as much, the absolute numbers of the poor continue to climb. Economic reforms create gainers and losers, but without a safety net the losers languish or sink deeper. So poverty reduction has been accompanied by increased inequality and insecurity.

Industrial reforms have unshackled entrepreneurship, reduced tariffs and taxes and helped increase competitiveness. But reforms have bypassed agriculture. And India's farmers have lost ground globally in terms of productivity and have become vulnerable to volatile global commodity prices, and rich country agricultural subsidies.

So we have the unfortunate juxtaposition that in the last five years, poverty rates reduced and farmer suicide rates mounted. It would be wrong to conclude, that we should go slow on reforms. The correct conclusion is to increase public investment in agriculture, remove barriers to a common countrywide economic market for agriculture, and increase the knowledge intensity in our farm sector.

The fight against poverty will require large ammunition which can only come from milching higher growth. By treating farmer suicides as a tip of the iceberg, we need a project tiger approach (tip of the ecology pyramid) in our fight against poverty.[31]

The crucial determinants of wealth and poverty are not differences in incentives, but differences in how people respond to them. In successful economies, people work hard, accumulate, and innovate even when their incentives are poor. In failed economies, people work little, save little, and stick with outmoded techniques even when incentives are good.

How can we transform the economic cultures of poor societies to be more like rich ones?

When workers move from a poor to a rich economy, there is rapid adaptation to the economic mores of the new society. In the textile industry in the early twentieth century, for example, output per worker hour of Polish workers in New England was four times greater than that of Polish workers using the same machines in Poland. One reason for illegal migration from the poor to the rich economies is many such migrants' ability to adapt to economic life in rich economies.[32]

Conventional business management principles rule out this solution. Unlike state service providers, business corporations have the luxury of segmenting markets and choosing those where they can make money. Indeed, to exit from loss-making segments and focus on profitable ones is good business strategy, since the poor cannot pay as much as rich people can, and since production and delivery of the small quantities the poor can buy is more costly, corporations are reluctant to serve them. Even public sector banks in India, when pushed to perform as well as private banks, feel handicapped by their obligation to serve the poor. The Planning Commission's approach paper to the Eleventh Plan says, a root cause of farmer's suicides is the failure of the banking system in extending credit that has led them to excessive dependence on informal sources of credit at exorbitant rates.

Economic reforms, as presently conceived, are directed towards the expansion of the scope of the private sector with the belief that investments and high returns in the corporate sector will improve the lives of the poor somehow. Perhaps all-round better reforms would be those that ensure that what is good for the country also becomes good for business corporations—reforms that induce the private sector to apply its inventiveness to serve the poor along with the rich.

India has a very unusual combination of a high performing private sector with enlightened business leaders as well as a democratically elected government that perforce are accountable to hundreds of millions of poor people. No other country has this potent combination—not China, nor the US, nor Sweden or the UK. India's leaders in the private and public sectors should not engage in sterile debates on socialism *versus* capitalism, nor imitate those countries. History is calling on them to work together, be innovative, and create a better model of inclusive development.[33]

A new World Bank study estimates that India's GDP could go up five times and the growth process becomes more inclusive if it could stimulate innovation in its economy. The Indian economy presents a mixed picture. There are some islands of excellence, which demonstrate potential. If standards and practices elsewhere could be scaled up to the best of what already exists, there would be an explosion of creativity and output as well as significant benefits for the poor.

There's a looming shortage in skills and talent. Despite having a predominantly young population and one of the largest systems of higher learning, India will face a deficit of half a million skilled workers by 2010.

Limited skills and training would no longer be a bottleneck for the economy if global best practices could be incorporated in education, but for that the education sector has to be deregulated and the welcome mat laid out for foreign universities. China understands the need for forcign universities to come to the county; more than 700 foreign academic programmes operate there now.

Besides raising the calibre of its schools and colleges, companies too could do a better job of offering in-house skills training to their employees. 92 per cent firms offer in-service training in China, against only a paltry 15 per cent in this country. Importantly, the government must put a series of policies in place to promote more research labs in the public as well as private sectors, encourage venture capitalists, create an enabling intellectual property and patent regime, and facilitate technology transfers. For India's economic miracle to happen it needs urgently to unleash innovation across the board, not in just a few sectors.[34]

THE JOBS CONUNDRUM

Growth is taking place with apparently too few additional jobs created. Unemployment is said to be multiplying in the countryside as agriculture stagnates. Arjun Sen Gupta's 'National Commission on Unorganised Enterprises' has reportedly calculated that over 800 million Indians live on less than Rs. 20 a day and nearly 400 million workers (86% of the labour force) work under "utterly deplorable conditions" and have "extremely few livelihood options".

One part of the answer to rural poverty lies in encouragement to small and marginal farmers to diversify from pure foodgrain production to combining it with high value crops. This will both reduce the displacement of farmers from agriculture to non-farm employment and will generate a significant number of jobs as more labour-intensive vegetable, spice and fruit cultivation are undertaken. Another part of the answer lies in engaging with the unorganised sector whose issues the national commission has attempted to address.

Off-farm enterprises are often derided as low-productivity activities with no future. Yet, it is well known that these activities not only provide more employment but also, in practice, continue to contribute more to GDP than does the shining IT sector. The fact is that there are substantial opportunities for value addition in the informal sector that remain untapped on account of information asymmetry, infrastructure deficiency and market distortions.

The question is how can these issues be addressed in practice; how can small farmers and unorganised enterprises be effectively linked to the market so as to take their rightful place in the modern economy? For decades, the government has talked of 'reviving' off-farm enterprises. For decades, budgetary allocations have been made and institutions such as the Small Farmers' Agribusiness Consortiums created to address the issues of market linkage that separate small cultivators from the market and limit the growth of unorganised enterprises. However, it is the common perception that, small successes aside, not much has been achieved. Yet, even now, anything from Rs. 4,000 crore to Rs. 10,000 crore of government funds are reportedly available for the promotion of micro-enterprises.

Here the answer lies not in creating more bureaucratic structures but in supporting existing local marketing arrangements and business service providers to become more effective. There are a number of organizations in different parts of the country promoting livelihoods in precisely this way. EDA Rural Systems (a development support organization in Gurgaon) is one such. In its honey livelihoods project in Bihar, EDA has helped to increase the productivity of local honey production by organizing technical programmes and to enhance the market strength of producers by (i) introducing the unique litchi flavour of local honey to traders nation-wide, increasing competition for local produce, (ii) organizing honey producers into associations have taken up collective bargaining with traders, and (iii) linking the associations with the Sudha Dairy (an NDDB affiliate) as bulk buyer and marketer of honey. Encouragement to local traders to establish honey processing plants has further increased local value addition. Honey producers' incomes have increased by 50 per cent or more while significant additional employment has been created—an estimated 6,000 new jobs in a sector originally employing about 2,000 people.[35]

The Administration of NREGS

The National Rural Employment Guarantee Act (NREGA) becomes redundant when actual choices are denied to people. The Act's emphasis on people's participation is not realized when people are not only turned away but face repression for fighting for their rights, when job cards and muster rolls are fudged and funds siphoned off. On the other hand, administrative costs are rising (Rs. 753 crore annually). Regular employment at a minimum wage is still the dream and the first demand of the poor. Though half-hearted, this extension has the potential to change the consumption pattern and share of rural economy, increase the bargaining power specially of women workers, finally leading to a change in the power equations in rural India—towards a more equitable socio-economic order.[36]

NREGS, if administered well, would be exactly the antidote to the 'jobless growth' problem. There is growth that is not percolating down to the poor, tax revenues are booming, and the best use of available public resources would be to provide jobs to the poor. Second, the additional expenditure should not be too large since the budget did provide a tidy sum for the implementation of SGRY (Sampoorna Grameen Rozgar Yojana) in the non-NREGA districts: NREGA is likely to effectively replace SGRY in those districts.

There are a few caveats, however. Being the 'flagship' scheme of the present government, it is sometimes being pushed too much. There are areas where market wages are higher than the wage rates fixed under the programme; such places would naturally exhibit little demand for it. But the strong pressure exerted to show 'good results' is a sure recipe for misutilization of funds. The happiest situation would be when no one would require jobs under this scheme. Since this is a demand-driven programme, targets should be a no-no unless they can be scientifically tailored to specific areas. Further, despite stronger safeguards, as compared to the earlier employment programmes, there are reports of inadequate awareness of implementation, as also leakage. These problems have to be looked into in detail and the loopholes plugged.[37]

The NREGA, 2005 guarantees 100 days of employment in a financial year to any rural house-hold whose adult members are willing to do unskilled manual work. The average days of work provided to rural households eligible under the National Rural Employment Guarantee Act (NREGA) was far lower than even 45 a year in most of the 330 districts it now operates in.

In fact, in some of the poorer states such as Bihar, the number of person-days of work actually done per rural household that demanded work was as low as 18.16. In another poor state, Assam the average person-days actually completed by rural households provided work up to September this year was 21.61 and in MP, the average rural household got to complete only 39.90 person-days of work up to

September 2007. The figure is much better in states such as Maharashtra (44.69 person-days) and Rajasthan (50.67 person-days) and Tamil Nadu (52.59 person-days per household) but these were the exceptions and did little to boost the national average. The NREGS is a demand-based and not budgetary allocation based programme, as the government so often likes to assert.

Orissa, among the poorer states in the country, managed to provide 100 days of work to 1,989 households through the year upto September 2007. Most of the households were from only three districts (Dhenkanal, Mayurbhanj, Sambalpur) out of those in which the NREGS is operative, although 4.23 lakh households were provided work (out of 4.46 lakh that demanded work). Some 135.94 lakh person-days of work were generated at an expenditure of Rs. 113.86 crore in the state and in August alone, 7,51,37 households were provided work. In impoverished Koraput district, only one household so far has completed 100 days of work and in Kalahandi, a grand total of 70 households have done so for the year. In Kandhamal, seven households have completed 100 days of work so far. In 12 other districts, not a single household has completed 100 days of work.[38]

Among all major States, Rajasthan comes first in terms of employment generation per rural household under the National Rural Employment Guarantee Act (NREGA). In 2006-07, the average rural household in Rajasthan's six "NREGA District" worked for as many as 77 days under this programme, earning nearly Rs. 4,000 in the process. This is an unprecedented achievement in the history of social security in India.

Further, disadvantaged sections of the population are the main gainers. The share of women in NREGA employment is around two-thirds in Rajasthan, and that of the Scheduled Caste and Scheduled Tribe households is as high as 80 per cent. In this and other ways, the Act contributes to social equity and economic redistribution.

Nevertheless, when a full-fledged social audit of the NREGA was conducted in Dungarpur district in Rajasthan, in 2006, low wage payments emerged as the main problem in an area where the Act was doing quite well otherwise. One year later, this problem persists.

There are also other problems with the NREGA in Rajasthan, such as the shortage of trained staff and lack of participatory planning. But the non-payment of minimum wages is a particularly serious lacuna, which calls for urgent investigation and redress. Extracting hard labour from poor people for as little of Rs. 23 a day is a serious violation of the Constitutional rights. This also threatens to defeat one of the basic purposes of the Employent Guarantee Act—the empowerment of labourers.[39]

A social audit of the functioning of the National Rural Employment Guarantee Scheme in Villupuram district in Tamil Nadu revealed that despite many problems it enhances transparency and accountability in governance and offers a lifeline to the rural poor.[40]

The NREGS appears to be heavily slanted against women. Participation of women in a scheme supposed to provide 100 days of employment in manual labour to every rural households has been found to be negligible.

A study conducted across 21 districts by the NGO PRIA (Society for Participatory Research in Asia) has found that only 1.01 per cent women in 24-Parganas in West Bengal, 3.9 per cent in Sirmour in Himachal Pradesh. 2.57 per cent in Sitapur in Uttar Pradesh and 13 per cent in Madhubani in Bihar had enrolled in this scheme.

Numbers of women are so low that in the five districts where the survey was conducted in both UP and Jharkhand, only 3,000 women had been enlisted in the muster rolls. In all, 3.91 per cent women in a 100 per cent literate state like Himachal Pradesh had enrolled for NREGA, while enrolment of women in Bihar was 13 per cent. The survey covered 14 states, including Madhya Pradesh, Andhra Pradesh, Himachal Pradesh, Haryana, Kerala, Orissa, Rajasthan, West Bengal, Uttar Pradesh and Jharkhand. What is ironical is that NREGA is being largely implemented by gram panchayats which have 33 per cent reservation for women members.

Almost half the surveyed households also complained that the minimum wages being paid to them were less than what had been prescribed. This was causing a great deal of disillusionment with the scheme and so many workers complained that given an option, they would not like to work under it.[41]

SUMMING UP

Select Action Points

1. Forging Ties with Private Entrepreneurs in Rural Areas

Lack of adequate and remunerative employment opportunities in rural areas has led to a large scale migration to the urban areas. The elasticity of employment in the agricultural sector has almost fallen to zero, thereby creating the need to look at other sectors for employment generation within the rural sector. While the employment options were abound for the skilled professionals, the periphery of the unskilled and semi-skilled was hit hard. This calls for an integrated approach involving the government, the private sector and the intended beneficiary—the local rural population. Enterprises in the rural areas require advice on technology-related aspects, on globally benchmarked production methods, information on the changing consumer needs and ways to diversify product portfolios.

Industry can partner with the panchayats to access and meet local requirements of agricultural inputs, to meet the storage and post-harvest needs, to engage in contract farming, to encourage direct procurement, to market agric produce and to promote agro processing. Each of these linkages has the potential to spur rural business in a major way.

2. Improvement in Infrastructure Facilities, Education Level and Health Standards

A strong push to economic activities in the rural areas required us to simultaneously improve infrastructure facilities and education levels and health standards among people residing in these areas. Efficient roads, power and telecom would serve to integrate fragmented rural economies with modern markets and, eventually, stem the tide of rural out migration and urban poverty.

A. Education

The existing education and training infrastructure cannot meet skilled manpower requirements. We need to begin from the primary school in villages and cities, work with underprivileged children and encourage them to get educated. We need to change our education system and focus on job-oriented courses. For a sharp focus on global talent development, education and vocational training have to be more market-driven.

While the sheen is unmistakable, we need to look deeper. After 60 years of Independence, our system does not ensure 'education for all' of the 200 million children in the age group of 6 to 14 years. 59 million children do not attend school in India. Even those who get educated are often not employable. India continues to add

10.8 million people to its population every year. This has serious implications for the education system as well. The experience of the last six decades needs to be utilized with care and caution. Without good quality education, the fruits of Independence will never reach the unaware and the ignorant. Education is the key to achieve social justice, equity, equality and human dignity. Any agenda for educational reforms must start by recognizing that children belong to a special category of citizens because they cannot protect their own rights. Children must be warmly hugged by the state in respect of all their needs, namely health and nutrition, safety, security, and education. Significant reforms in governance are required to ensure that the efforts to be made by different departments come together. This is not easy, but there is no alternative to evolve a child-centred system of governance so that India stops wasting its huge human resource potential on account of malnutrition, illiteracy, and child abuse. With widespread low haemoglobin levels and frequent illness, especially among girls, India cannot compete with its neighbours like China and Japan, let alone the Europeans and the Americans. For greater focus and efficiency in the delivery of child-related services, the entrenched Centre-State impasse must be overcome. While no one can deny the Centre's role in setting policy goals and providing funds for systemic reform, we can hardly overlook the lack of rigour and accountability in the States' response to policy directions. One glaring evidence is that 40 years after the Kothari Commission wrote its laudable report, even the pattern of stages it recommended has not been implemented in all the States. Adoption of the National Curriculum Framework, 2005, though it has the approval of CABE and has been implemented by CBSE, presents a similar story.

B. Healthcare

Although the availability of quality healthcare services has no doubt improved with the development of world-class hospitals supported by excellent doctors and the proliferation of diagnostic and pathology centres providing services on-line, this largely remains an urban phenomenon.

The underprivileged sections of the society are still deprived of even primary care due to either lack of infrastructure or funds. The challenge is to cater to these people who are fighting with life everyday. To make this dream a reality, the onus lies equally on the private and public sector to work out innovative models that marry the strengths of the two.

In spite of the government spending close to 6 per cent of the GDP on healthcare, the Indian public health system at the state level remains inadequate. It is time we looked at ways of infusing new life into this sector by providing it with incentives, benevolent tax structures, etc. that are accorded to infrastructure, IT, hotel and tourism. This will fast forward the much-awaited healthcare revolution in our country.

The linkages of child malnutrition with women's health and well-being are strong. Reducing child malnutrition requires enhancing women's freedoms and promoting gender equality. At the same time, the focus has also to shift from enhancing incomes and food availability to understanding how members of a household establish command over food, health and care. It is important to understand how family members acquire and apply knowledge on child caring and rearing practices, allocate time to look after children, and protect the cleanliness of the environment. But, above all, India's high levels of child malnutrition reflect the continuing neglect of health, the inadequate reach and efficacy of health and child care services, and the failure of strategies to reach the newborn children and those under the age of three. These deficiencies need to be addressed immediately.

3. Micro-savings and Financial Inclusion

For the poor households, which lack access to the formal insurance system and to a lesser extent the credit system, savings provide a safety net and help them tide over crises. Savings can also keep them away from the clutches of moneylenders, make formal institutions more favourable to lending to them, encourage investment and make them shift to more productive activities, as they may invest in slightly more risky activities which have an overall higher rate of return.

The poor even if they want to save, do not have an account to save in or a place to keep it in their small house stashed away somewhere. Integrating the need for savings and credit facility will benefit the poor and also make the activity more viable for banks and encourage them to lend to the poor.

The present thinking on savings by the poor presupposes that they are risk averse and prone to shocks, and that security, liquidity and the accessibility of their savings are important determinants of savings. Some banks, and micro finance institutions in the international context, have sought to respond to this by having a diversified portfolio of services tailored to the demand and they do manage to increase the saving and also the lending base.

Some of the steps suggested to make the policy of financial inclusion a success are:

- ❖ Financial inclusion should focus on the saving needs along with the credit needs.
- ❖ Have a diversified product portfolio for the poor but recognize that self-control problems need to be addressed by having commitment devices, and accordingly offer products with these features also. The products with commitment features should be optional.
- ❖ Out down transaction costs for the poor, by making innovative use of technology available and offering mobile vans with ATM and deposit collection features. These vans could visit the village periodically, say one in every two weeks. To test the external validity of the study by Ashraf, Karlan, and Yin (2005), the RBI should carry out a pilot study to establish the impact of various products on savings and borrowing. It should also study the economics of the scheme if services like mobile vans or for other deposit collection methods are established.[42]

People-friendly, responsive banking system with lesser formalities and paperwork, reaching out of the 232,913 village panchayats is the only way to supplant the usurious lending class. This can be supplemented by strengthened self-help groups (SHGs) in every panchayat. The SHGs are working successfully in many parts. Banks which are lending money for agriculture must have outlets to procure their products. That is the best way to help the poor farmers. The banks can work out a detailed system for it. One 21st century way to enhance financial inclusion is to use high technology (biometric smart cards, cellphones, low-cost ATMs) and mobile "business correspondents". BASIX is trying this in a pilot with the UTI Bank in East Delhi slums and Bihar villages. If this works, the RBI needs to vigorously replicate this and leave moneylenders alone.

4. Water Sector Reform

Subsidized access to water for economic and commercial purposes can no longer be sustained. The ground water situation is becoming critical. Ground water meets half of all irrigation needs besides 85 per cent of rural and 50 per cent of the urban water supply. But a quarter of all blocks surveyed by the Central Ground Water Board are now classified as critical, semi-critical, or overexploited. Unsustainable ground water extraction coupled with profligate use by the affluent is causing distress in urban areas. Water sector reform has become an imperative but there is no agreement on what will achieve optimal results. The expert group of the Planning Commission on groundwater headed by Dr. Kirit S. Parikh has pointed to the limited value of regulation in curbing extraction in a country with millions of wells. A massive community-led programme to recharge ground water and augment surface storage may perform better.

Agriculture accounts for a major part of all water use and any savings achieved through higher efficiency can ease the pressure on ground water, especially in the peninsular States.

Inefficient use in irrigation is partly blamed on the availability of free or highly subsidized power. Any attempt to make changes to this politically sensitive scheme is bound to run into trouble and the benefits to the ground water table may be modest. Better results can be achieved by strengthening subsidies for efficient micro-irrigation techniques, with concurrent support for rain harvesting and artificial recharge structures. In cities and towns, the value of mandatory rainwater harvesting to recharge ground water is tremendous—as is evident from the Central experience. As demand rises and supply comes under strain, the Centre, the States, and local bodies will be under pressure to exercise their authority as public trustees of water to guarantee equity and accessibility. In fact, courts have pinpointed this responsibility in cases involving ground water and river basin pollution in Tamil Nadu and unbridled extraction for profit in Kerala. The task of evolving a framework to meet the egalitarian objectives of the National Water Policy and the National Environment Policy must be taken up as a top priority.[43]

5. Rural Business Hubs

The Union Panchayati Raj Ministry is taking an initiative to develop one rural business hub in every block.

The initiative works on a win-win business relationship between the rural producers and the members of industry, facilitated by the panchayats. So far 99 MoUs have been signed across the states of Tamil Nadu (51), Karnataka (27), Uttarakhand (11), Rajasthan (4), Haryana (3), Nagaland (2) and Uttar Pradesh (1) in such diverse fields as food-processing, power generation and distribution, Jatropha plantation, carpet-weaving, handicrafts and stone-carving. These MoUs are at different stages of implementation.

SPOT

The objective of the latest initiative of the Union Panchayati Raj Ministry is to promote rural business hubs across the country by bringing to the attention of the business houses, both in the public and private sectors, the unique products or skills in each development block deriving from local resource endowment.

In November 2004, the Ministry of Panchayati Raj organized a national presentation on Rural Business Hubs, which was attended by 1,000 representatives of panchayats and 200 representatives of the Confederation of Indian Industry (CII). Joint RBH Council under the co-chairmanship of the Panchayati Raj Minister and the then CII president, was set up at the national level. Similar councils have been set up in 15 states. In consultation with the state government and panchayats, the Panchayati Raj Ministry has identified local resources and skills in more than 1,000 blocks, to develop and promote public-private-panchayat partnership, in which the panchayats will facilitate convergence of extant schemes of the state and Central Government.[44]

6. Controlling Floods in Eastern India

The government must recognize that the problem of recurrent floods in eastern India cannot be tackled without the cooperation of Nepal, Bhutan and Bangladesh, upper and lower riparian nations. For example, Nepal can initiate afforestation in its upper catchment area to impede excess water flow into eastern UP and north Bihar, while India helps it exploit much more than the present measly 8 per cent of its 43,000 MW hydel potential. India should also consider other avenues of ecological collaboration like soil conservation, agro-forestry and grassland and watershed management with Nepal. India would, in fact, do well to take the lead to evolve a consensus to put in place a holistic flood control programme for the entire south Asian region.

7. Reinventing Local Bodies

Way back in 1993 our Constitution was amended (73rd and 74th Amendments). The task of providing basic amenities, viz. roads, water supply, public health, sanitation, waste management, environment, culture, education, slum improvement, gardens, street lights etc. is now assigned to urban and rural local bodies like municipal corporations and gram panchayats, which form the third tier of the government, the first two being the central and state governments.

Although it is mandatory, the state governments are extremely reluctant to devolve functions, finances and functionaries to the local bodies. Not only that, they have created overlapping authorities like metropolitan development boards, water boards, slum rehabilitation authorities, housing boards, electricity boards, school boards, state road development corporations etc. leaving only garbage removal as possibly the sole exclusive responsibility of local bodies. Naturally, they are unable to carry out their constitutionally assigned duties of providing basic civic amenities and make India liveable.

The combined budgets of the central and state governments are Rs. 13 lakh crore. Half of this amount is required in the hands of the local bodies to make India liveable (presently only 7% is available). But how can the central and state governments transfer such vast sum of money to the local bodies when they are running huge fiscal deficits themselves? The answer lies in trimming these governments to their core responsibilities.

The Central Government has 46 ministries, whereas Japan has only 10 and the United States has only 15. Even state governments (e.g. Maharashtra) have 40-odd ministries. The tie has come when the Central Government should confine itself to the tasks that the Constitution of India has assigned to it, viz. defence, foreign affairs, etc. and providing viability gap funding for mega infrastructural projects like international airports, nuclear power plants etc. Similarly, the state governments should confine themselves to what the Constitution of India has assigned to them, viz. law and order, university education, ecology etc. and viability gap funding of infrastructure projects like roads, irrigation, electric power and special economic zones. What local bodies can do the central or state government should not do.

When central and state governments shed their non-core responsibilities, they will need just Rs. 250,000 crore to carry out their core functions (defence, foreign affairs, law and order, administration etc.). Another Rs. 300,000 crore can be earmarked for viability gap funding for infrastructure (power, roads, airports etc.). After providing for interest on government borrowings a whopping Rs. 500,000 crore can be transferred to local bodies. Local bodies should raise at least Rs. 100,000 crore through local taxes and user charges so that they have a total of Rs. 600,000 crore to spend. And they should spend it to make India liveable.

Urban local bodies should use these funds for urban renewal (mass transit, roads, flyovers, parking, water supply, garbage collection, slum improvement, playgrounds, street lights etc.). Rural local bodies should use these funds for rural renewal (watershed development, irrigation, sanitation, bio-energy and solar energy, primary and secondary education, primary health centres, food processing, good storage etc.). These functions are detailed out in the 11th and 12th Schedules to our Constitution.

But many urban local bodies do not have the wherewithal to speedily execute such activities. So we should focus on private-public partnership. A number of cities have shown us the way. Indore has introduced a 50-50 scheme where citizens in a locality get their roads revamped from a private contractor and municipal corporation foots 50 per cent of the bill. Ahmednagar has privatized bus transport and octroi collection. Surat, once afflicted by plague, has become *khoobsoorat* (beautiful) and so the local citizens do not mind paying high property taxes. Ralegan Sindhi, a village in Maharashtra has blazed a new trail in rainwater harvesting and so on.

Most of the rural local bodies possess neither the skills, nor the resources, nor the manpower to execute such activities. Yet they ought to be involved in deciding the scope of rural renewal. 'Top down' approach would fail because it would not value local knowledge and initiative.

Rural local bodies should appoint consulting firms to discuss with the stakeholders to prepare detailed projects reports.[45]

Biodiversity Management

Gram sabhas can coordinate with the Biodiversity Management Committee, created under the Biological Diversity Act, 2002, to document the biodiversity resources being conserved, sustainably used and managed by it under the Scheduled Tribes and other Traditional Forest Dwellers (Recognition of Forest Rights) Act, 2006.

The draft rules to the Tribal Rights Act also empower the gram sabhas to record individual, group or community knowledge associated with such biodiversity and cultural diversity and voluntarily disclosed information furnished by knowledge providers.

This documentation shall be the property of the gram sabha and it will decide on which of its parts or contents are to be made freely available to the public and the terms and conditions under which other parts or contents may be disclosed to the parties.

The gram sabha can coordinate with the State Biodiversity Boards as well as the Protected Plant Varieties and Farmers' Rights Authority in the management of such documented knowledge to promote assertion of intellectual property rights and ensure equitable sharing of benefits from its use. The gram sabha will regulate access to biodiversity resources by outsiders and to levy collection charges and work out benefit sharing arrangements.

When a right of access to biodiversity and community right to intellectual property and traditional knowledge related to biodiversity and cultural diversity has been recognized, it will include rights to regulate access, control, develop and protect traditional science and technology associated with biodiversity resources including genetic resources, seeds, medicines, health practices, medicinal plants, agriculture, knowledge of flora and fauna, minerals and other indigenous knowledge systems, and practices, according to the draft rules.

As far as the duties of the holders of forest rights are concerned, the draft rules empower the gram sabhas to perform the duties on behalf of the holders, and the duties include preparing a plan for the protection and management of community forest resources, sanctuaries and national parks; biodiversity and watershed management plans.

The gram sabha will guide functioning of the Joint Forest Management Committee, the Eco-development Committee, the Biodiversity Management Committee or any such institution.[46]

FOOTNOTES

1. "Chasing the Monsoon: Irrigation can cut dependence on rains", editorial, *The Economic Times* (Kolkata: 26.5.2007), p. 8.
2. "Reform India Water Sector: To check groundwater depletion", editorial, *The Economic Times* (Kolkata: 27.6.2007), p. 8.
3. Kar, Indrani "Incentives should not be seen as giveaways", *The Economic Times* (Kolkata: 14.5.2007), p. 13.
4. Joshi, P. K. "Ensure Corporates share benefits with farmers", *The Economic Times* (Kolkata: 14.5.2007), p. 13.
5. "Food Chain: Government moots Private sector tie-up with farmer cooperatives", editorial, *The Times of India* (Patna-Ranchi: 29.5.2007), p. 16.
6. Jagannathan, Prabha "Agri-growth central to overall prosperity: SEZ lobby dumping farm sector's genuine concerns", *The Economic Times* (Kolkata: 10.9.2007), p. 13.
7. Gulati, Ashok: "How can India reform its fertilizer policy?", *The Economic Times* (Kolkata: 21.8.2007), p. 9.
8. Avasthi, U.S., *Ibid.*
9. Joshi, Sharad, *Ibid.*
10. Goyal, Prashant, "Signals from futures", *The Economic Times* (Kolkata: 6.9.2007), p. 8.
11. "Farmers share experience of organic agriculture", *The Asian Age* (New Delhi: 7.10.2007), p. 4.
12. Venkataraman, N.S. "Agro-chemicals: Missed Chances", *The Economic Times* (Kolkata: 18.8.2007), p. 6.
13. Gupta, Ravi "Mandatory 10% ethanol blending?: The Concern over shortages is Unfounded", *The Economic Times* (Kolkata: 3.9.2007), p. 14.
14. Sharma, Praveen "Managing Risk in Agriculture", *The Economic Times* (Kolkata 24.8.2007), p. 4.
15. "Health for Wealth", editorial, *The Times of India* (Patna-Ranchi: 7.9.2007), p. 10.
16. "Maternal Mortality Challenges", editorial, *The Hindu* (New Delhi: 10.7.2007), p. 8.
17. Shiva Kumar, A.K. "Why are levels of child malnutrition high?", *The Hindu* (New Delhi: 22.6.2007), p. 10.
18. Sharma, Kalpana "The Invisible Half", *The Hindu* (New Delhi: 7.10.2007), p. 3.

19. Sinha, Amarjeet "Craft a credible public health system", *The Economic Times* (Kolkata: 27.2.2007), p. 6.
20. Reddy, Sangeeta "Go in for US/UK healthcare model?", *The Economic Times* (Kolkata: 27.2.2007), p. 6.
21. Singh, Malvinder Mohan "Healthcare needs radical thinking", *The Economic Times* (Kolkata: 27.2.2007), p. 6.
22. Rajput, J. S. "Education 60: Results don't match expectations", *The Asian Age* (New Delhi: 15.8.2007), p. 6.
23. Pawar, Rajendra S. "Educate the Masses," *The Times of India* (Patna-Ranchi: 9.10.2007), p. 16.
24. Mukherjee, Amitabh "Science education in India", *The Hindu* (New Delhi: 16.8.2007), p. 9.
25. Rajput, J.S. "Who will teach the teachers?", *The Asian Age* (New Delhi: 12.9.2007), p. 6.
26. Kumar, Krishna "Between Progress and Reluctance," *The Hindu* (New Delhi: 24.8.2007), p. 10.
27. Stiglitz, Joseph E. "The challenge is to make more people participate in India's growth", *The Asian Age* (New Delhi: 9.1.2007), p. 7.
28. "Forward with reforms: Time to translate blueprint into action", editorial, *The Economic Times* (Kolkata: 10.10.2006), p. 6.
29. "Rags and Riches: A profile of the face of Indian Poverty", editorial, *The Times of India* (Mumbai: 18.8.2007), p. 16.
30. Sen, Chiranjib "No automatic link between growth and poverty", *The Economic Times* (Kolkata: 28.3.2007), p. 12.
31. Ranade, Ajit "We need a 'Project Tiger' to fight Poverty", *The Economic Times* (Kolkata: 28.3.2007), p. 12.
32. Clark, Gregory "The wealth and culture of nations", *The Economic Times* (Kolkata: 8.10.2007), p. 17.
33. Maira, Arun "Competitiveness and growth via inclusion", *The Economic Times* (Kolkata: 10.10.2006), p. 6.
34. "How to Get Rich: Stimulate innovation to win the future", editorial, *The Times of India* (Patna-Ranchi: 6.10.2007), p. 14.
35. Sinha, Sanjay "Livelihood in times of growth", *The Economic Times* (Kolkata: 29.9.2007), p. 7.
36. Dhuru, Arundhati "Should NREGS Cover all 600 districts?: Its implementation stymies the objectives", *The Economic Times* (Kolkata: 3.10.2007), p. 14.

37. Sen, Tapas K. "Should NREGS cover all 600 districts?: It could be the antidote to jobless growth", *The Economic Times* (Kolkata: 3.10.2007), p. 14.
38. Jagannathan, Prabha "NREGS dream may turn sour......", *The Economic Times* (Kolkata: 2.10.2007), p. 7.
39. Dreze, Jean and Siddhartha Lal "Employment guarantee: Unfinished agenda", *The Hindu* (New Delhi: 13.7.2007), p. 11.
40. Lakshman, Nirmala "The hundred days basket", *The Hindu* (New Delhi: 14.8.2007), p. 81.
41. Sehgal, Rashme "Job scheme discriminates against women", *The Asian Age* (New Delhi: 3.10.2007), p. 4.
42. Ahuja, Manoj "Micro-saving & financial inclusion", *The Economic Times* (Kolkata: 27.7.2007), p. 6.
43. "Using groundwater wisely", editorial, *The Hindu* (New Delhi: 9.10.2007), p. 10.
44. Parsa, Venkat "Rural Business Hubs in all districts soon", *The Asian Age* (New Delhi: 7.9.2007), p. 4.
45. Firodia, Arun "Reinvent government to make India liveable", *The Economic Times* (Kolkata: 6.8.2007), p. 17.
46. Dhar, Aarti "Gram sabhas can coordinate with biodiversity panel", *The Hindu* (New Delhi: 28.9.2007), p. 9.

Index